THE

BATTLEFIELD

DEAD

by
Elizabeth Matusiak

i

Published by

STATE OF THE ART, LTD.

**4942 Morrison Road
Denver, CO 80219**
*303-936-1978
Fax 303-936-1770*

THE BATTLEFIELD DEAD
by Elizabeth Matusiak

Copyright © 2000

First printing 2000

ISBN: 0-930161-53-X

Published by:
State of the Art, Ltd.
4942 Morrison Road
Denver, Colorado 80219
303-936-1978
Fax 303-936-1770

iii

Ed and Elizabeth Matusiak as they portray General Winfield
Scott Hancock and his wife, Almira, at a re-enactment of
The Battle Of Gettysburg.

ABOUT THE AUTHOR

My husband Ed and I lived in Edgewater Park, New Jersey all of our lives. We traveled twice a month to Gettysburg. In April of 1998, Ed retired. That day, we left New Jersey to find a home in Gettysburg.

On May 14, 1998 we owned our own home in Gettysburg. We have been here for a year and a half and intend to spend the rest of our lives in this enchanting area. In death we intend to sleep in our beloved Gettysburg forever.

Elizabeth and Ed portray General Winfield S. Hancock and his wife, Almira.

DEDICATION

This book is dedicated to my husband and children, who have traveled back and forth to the battlefields with me. They have felt embarrassed as I discussed my ghostly encounters but, still stood by my side as I collected the material for this book. Also, I would like to thank all of those who shared their amazing encounters with me, which made this book possible.

INTRODUCTION

Having family and friends in Gettysburg gave me the opportunity to learn and study the "BATTLEFIELD".

I spent every summer with my aunt and uncle in Gettysburg and could not get enough of the "CIVIL WAR". My fascination with this war often baffled me.

After attending Oregon State University, I was confused as to what I wanted to do with my life.

I married and raised my four children but, I never lost that calling to go back to Gettysburg.

I studied the BATTLEFIELDS and the war for years and could go up against the best historians, but that wasn't my calling.

What struck my interest was the people who confided in me their stories of the unexplained encounters they were having. I found that our brothers and sisters of the South spoke very freely of their ghostly encounters.

They are a warm and friendly lot and it often bothers me that we fought againt such lovely people.

I have many stories of "The Southern Battlefields" but, I wish to focus my first book on my beloved Gettysburg.

I would like to add that after going to see the renouned and interesting Karyol Kirkpatrick, I have a better understanding of my feelings. After a reading with Karyol, she told me I nursed the wounded in the "Civil War" and that could be my emotional tie with this ungodly battle.

AUTHORS NOTES

To my readers I would like to say, please don't come to Gettysburg for the spirits.

Some may see one or even two ghosts or hear strange and unusual things but, there are many who haven't seen or heard a thing.

If you visit the battlefields, do so for the history of the brave men who gave their lives gallantly for a cause that they believed in.

Let us learn our history so it can never repeat itself, therefore, the innocent lives of men and boys will not be in vain.

If you would like to order a copy of
"The Battlefield Dead"
please send this order form along with your payment of $9.95
plus $3.50 for shipping and handling (Denver Colorado
residence add 7.3% tax) per book to:

STATE OF THE ART, LTD.
4942 MORRISON ROAD
DENVER, CO 80219
303-936-1978
FAX   303-936-1770

SEND TO:

Name_____

Address_____

City_____State_____Zip_____

Phone_(_____)_____

Number of Copies_____

Amount enclosed_____

Have You Had An Encounter With The Ghosts Of The Battlefields?

I am always ready to listen to tales and view pictures about the ghost encounters on the Battlefields. If you have had an encounter that you would like to share please call me or send your experiences and photographs to:

Elizabeth Matusiak
90 Knight Road, Lot 22
Gettysburg, PA 17325-8759
717-338-0365

Please enclose the following information so that we may contact you for permission to publish your tales and pictures.

Name:_____

Address:_____

City:_____

State:_____Zip:_____

Phone:_____

CONTENTS

ABOUT THE AUTHOR	iv,v
DEDICATION	vi
INTRODUCTION	vii
AUTHORS NOTES	viii
ORDER FORM	ix
PERMISSION SHEET	xi
THEY STILL SING	1
FACT OR FICTION	7
ONE LEGGED YANK	9
HIS SWORD	11
I HEARD DRUMS	13
MY GHOSTLY ENCOUNTER	14
HITCHING A RIDE	19
PULLED BACK IN TIME	21
POEM	22
THE AMERICAN FLAG	23
THE GENERAL	25
POEM	27

CONTENTS
(continued)

YES...THEY STILL ROAM   29

POEM   31

SOMBER FEELINGS   33

THREE WOUNDED YANKS   35

BAG PIPES   37

JOSHUA   41

CANNON FIRE   43

THE HEADLESS SOUL   45

UNSEEN BOOTS   47

POEM   49

THREE WOUNDED REBELS   51

WHISPER   55

THE DEN   57

A PAIR OF REBELS   61

THE PEACE LIGHT   65

THE FOG   67

POEM   70

THE ROCKING CHAIR   71

CONTENTS
(continued)

THE DARK MAN   73

THE SHADOW   75

OVER AND OVER AGAIN   77

THE BUTTERNUT SOLDIER   79

A RE-ENACTOR?   81

POEM   83

THE STATUE   85

THE SHORT RIDE   87

POEM   88

THE LANTERNS   89

THE GHOSTLY BRIGADE   91

SACH'S BRIDGE   93

POEM   97

HE MARCHED ALONE   99

THE CAMPGROUND GHOST   101

NIGHT RIDER   103

THE PLAYFUL SPIRIT   105

REINCARNATION   109

TWO MORE REBELS   111

CONTENTS
(continued)

POEM	112
THE FOOT FETISH	113
THE 7TH NEW JERSEY	117
ORBS	121
POEM	124
ORBS OF MY OWN	125
POEM	128
POEM	132
POEM	136
KARYOL KIRKPATRICK	137
POEM	140
THROUGH A CHILD'S EYES	143

THEY STILL SING

It was a perfect night for a ghost hunt. The moon was full and the fog lay covering the ground. I neither saw nor heard anything but, the feeling of dread filled me. Could I do this?

Finally, my curiosity overcame my fear. However, I must add that I never went on these ghost quests alone. I always managed to drag some poor soul along with me.

On this particular occasion, I had my Uncle Walt with me. There was no way I was going to the George Armstrong Custer Monument alone to put a tape recorder on it. I must say, it was pretty eerie. The fog was at our feet, swirling around as we walked. Putting the tape up there was spooky enough, but the thought of coming back later to retrieve it was petrifying to comprehend.

Finally, after that mission was accomplished, we proceeded to the other side of the field where the Rebels fought, to sit and wait for our tape to play through. The road was very narrow and winding with woods and farmland all around.

We were almost to the spot where General Fitzhugh Lee, (Robert E. Lee's nephew), the tar heels and the Virginians of Colonel John Chambless had their cannons placed.

As we approached the corner, Uncle Walt stopped the truck and peered behind him. Asking what was wrong, he replied, "I just saw a tall man standing over there by those cannons."

Thinking that it was a Park Ranger, we both looked behind us. We saw nothing but the light of the moon.

He repeated, "I know I saw someone standing there, I saw him as the headlights passed over."

At that point I had no doubt that he had seen someone or something, for he was not a true believer in the supernatural. When I asked him to describe exactly what he saw, he said he really couldn't make out the man's features, only that he was very tall.

We parked the truck across from Gen. Fitz. Lee's cannons, where we waited for our tape to finish. I was thinking about what Uncle Walt had seen and I could not come up with a logical reason for a Ranger to be standing in the middle of a dark Battlefield alone. While sitting there, I felt a cold chill and such a feeling of depression that I suddenly felt sad and all alone. I saw nothing in front of me; the dark was so thick I could barely see Uncle Walt's face.

The clouds were covering the moon and I nearly jumped out of my skin when he yelled, "Wow!" "I just got the coldest chill." He had no sooner said that when we heard a yell that sounded Southern . . . right at the truck window. Needless to say, we took off like scared rabbits. We were driving a bit faster than we should have but, we slowed down about a quarter of a mile away. We stopped again and sat with the lights off and the windows down, our hearts racing out of our chests and listened.

We were only parked there a few minutes, when once again, at the same window, a voice screamed "Heeeelp!" in an eerie Southern drawl.

I'll tell you this, I saw nothing there but, I heard its eerie cry. So, once again, we high tailed it out of there. We suddenly remembered the tape that we had put on the monument, so we had to back track to retrieve it. When we arrived at Custer's Monument, we had to seam up all of our nerve just to walk up and get the tape. We ran up to that monument just as fast as our feet would carry us, and the whole time I prayed that the Reb would stay on his side of the Battlefield, as he was far beyond any help that I could give him.

Our experience with the Rebel yell was frightening enough but, we soon found out just how much more astonishing our situation was going to become.

When we got back to the campground, we listened to our tape. At first, we only heard the night sounds of frogs and crickets. Then suddenly we heard the sound of horses galloping. I knew instantly that it was the sound of horse hooves. We rewound the tape three time to listen to it over and over. We looked at each other in surprise. We were both trembling with fear and excitement. As soon as we gained our composer, we heard the sound of rapid gunfire.

Within minutes, we heard the sound of many men singing. We couldn't make out the words but, we knew it was a gallant song. Although I have read, watched and heard many ghost stories of the main Battlefield in town, I hadn't heard of any out here. People didn't know of the goings on in this field.

I have spent many days studying the field of death and have noticed a few cars with visitors passing through in the day but never at night. Many died here, as J.E.B. Stuart and George Custer clashed swords in this now peaceful place. Yet, in the blood drenched fields, "They Still Sing."

Fitz Lee's Cannons

The Loop that circles around the battlefield.

Fitz Lee-Robert E. Lee's Nephew, Rebel side of Cavalry Field.

Colonel Purnell, Maryland Cavalry

FACT OR FICTION

Many people claim to have seen these active ghosts of the past, whether it is Johnny Reb or Billy Yank. Day or night, rain or shine, it doesn't matter. They always seem to show up. I have found that taping is better at night. The daytime visitors and traffic sounds seem to drown out any sounds of the supernatural. However, there have also been many sightings during broad daylight. Sylvia Archer told me of her visit to East Cavalry field. There were no other visitors around at the time, only her husband and herself. They stood looking over the lush fields of corn and beans. As they proceeded to walk up to General Custer's Monument, she looked toward Maryland Monument and saw a Yankee officer standing there. He wore a thick brimmed, black hat and his coat came to his knees to meet his high black boots. She even saw the double row of gold buttons on his coat. She remembered thinking what a gorgeous looking man he was, with his dark hair and long beard. She turned around to see if her husband saw him as well but, when she turned back, he was gone. They were standing in an open field and she wondered how he could have gotten away so quickly. She couldn't explain where he went.

She didn't think she was experiencing an apparition because she saw him too clearly as he leaned against the Maryland Monument. She claimed to have seen him so clear that she could have drawn a picture of him. Her husband never saw anything. They both remember the distinct odor of a cigar.

The officers of the Civil War were prone to smoking cigars and many visitors have caught the brief smell of cigar smoke. A few people have told me that they have had their cameras malfunction while trying to take a picture of the Maryland Monument. The Maryland Cavalry made a charge led by General Custer against J.E.B. on July 3, 1863 on this field.

Civil War Hospital

ONE LEGGED YANK

Knowing the history of the Civil War hospital makes me very happy that I was born in the 20th century.

Once a soldier was shot in any limb, it was immediately amputated. That was the only cure for "What ailed you." The suffering was ghastly. When wounds became infected in the summer heat, the only treatment was a rag soaked in water and placed over the wound. Many wounds became infected and were crawling with maggots. Legs, feet, toes, arms and fingers were piled as high as the hospital windows. There is no doubt as to why there have been so many sightings here in Gettysburg.

Two friends of mine, Jean and Alice Cates told me a story so sad I could almost picture this young boy's misery upon his face. While they were walking down Taneytown Road one warm evening, the two sisters had nothing on their minds except the party they were going to attend over the weekend.

A ghostly encounter was the furthest thing from their minds; they did not believe in such things.

They were almost to the hospital along Taneytown Road when they heard a loud moaning. When they looked in the direction of the sound, they saw a Yankee soldier. They looked closer and not believing what they were seeing, they noticed how dirty his face looked, as if it were smeared with black soot.

Alice related how sad he looked, as if he were trying to cry out in sorrow.

The thing that scared them out of their wits was when they noticed his legs. He stood before them with only one. The other had the pant leg cut away, leaving only a bloody stub exposed.

As they ogled at the young Yank, he softly moaned and faded away.

Alice and Jean do not remember how long they stood there mesmerized. They felt as though they were waking from a dream. They turned to face each other as if to verify what they had just experiences. They both simply nodded to each other and continued on with their walk, but this time at a much quicker pace. After hearing their strange episode, I asked them how they felt about what they had seen. Jean explained that they believed that when you die, you sleep until Resurrection Day.

Never expecting to see a spirit, they left wondering just what had occurred. Although they know that it was a Yankee soldier, minus one leg, ragged and dirty, alone and sad, they still are not ready to admit that they had an encounter with the spirit world.

HIS SWORD

My husband and I made a weekend trip to Gettysburg to take a few pictures to add to this book.

I was taking a picture of the creek J.E.B. Stuart crossed on his way to that great clash with George Custer. Two of the neighbors came out and started a very stimulating conversation. We were so intrigued by what these lovely people had to say that we completely forgot to ask their names. I am not one to pass up an opportunity for a good ghost story. Their story had my undivided attention.

They told me that two of the locals were relic hunting on some farmland that was privately owned. They both had the feeling that they were being watched, so they turned around and to their utter surprise, they saw a Yankee officer with sword in hand, raised high above his head. They turned to each other, both asking the same question; "Do you know him?" Both answering, "No, do you?"

When they turned back around to where the officer stood, they found no one was there. They decided to go talk to the landowner to see if he had let someone else onto the property.

After finding out that they where the only two out there, they decided to investigate. They returned to the spot where they saw the intruder and when they looked down, they saw the sword that he had held above his head, stuck snuggly into the earth.

To this day, these two gentlemen still hold this precious treasure in their collection.

This is to the thanks of this unearthly visitor, who for some reason, wanted his sword to be found.

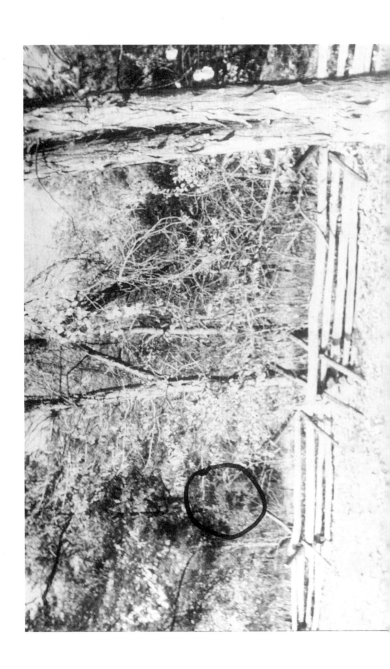

Taken on Wheatfield Road after hearing men talking softly. Below is a face with a mustache and cap.

I HEARD DRUMS

Sylvia Archer told me an interesting story. She saw a Union soldier standing by the Maryland Monument while she and her husband, Lou, visited Gettysburg in June of 1995. When she returned home, she related to her mother, Sylvia Ackers, what she had encountered.

She was very sympathetic to what her daughter was telling her and after seeing how sincere she was, she planned her own trip to Gettysburg, with high hopes that she too would encounter something from the spirit world as well.

This is when I had the opportunity to meet these two wonderful and fun loving women. Although fun loving, they were very serious about their ghost hunting. I met the pair one day while I was sitting on a rock at the Wheatfield, thinking of the dead Yanks that made this place a carpet of blue.

We struck up a conversation and I learned that they were from New Jersey as well as I. They seemed very inquisitive about the battle so, I shared some of my knowledge of the battlefield. Our conversation drifted to East Cavalry Field.

They explained that they had gone out there the previous night. Mrs. Archer confided in me her tale of 1995, and why they both were really there.

Getting very excited about telling me of the experience the previous night and talking very fast, they explained how they were sitting in their car at East Cavalry Field and they distinctly heard the sound of drums. As they sat there, the drums seemed to be coming closer and closer. Then they heard this ungodly screaming. That was enough, they got themselves out of there.

After leaving the battlefield, they went back to their motel room. They couldn't sleep because they kept going over and over the sound of that unearthly scream. They explained to me that the drums sounded very much like those they have heard in re-enactments. I asked them if I could use their story in my book and they were both more than obliged. To my added delight, they offered me two pictures that they had taken at the Wheatfield and at Devil's Den. They are presented among the pictures in this book.

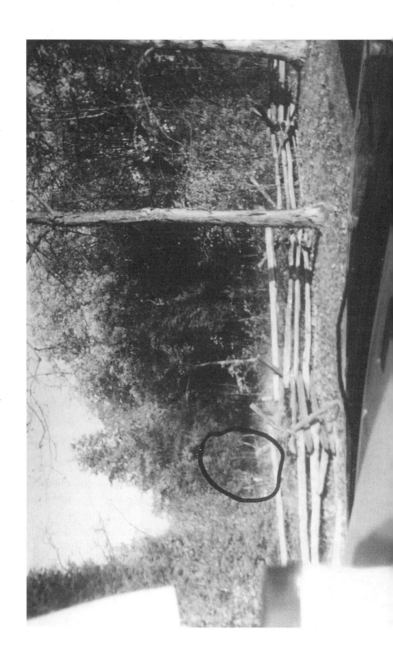

Below is the form of a man, taken by Sylvia Archer.

MY GHOSTLY ENCOUNTER

For years now I have worked diligently on collecting many interesting stories of the paranormal. I have spent many hours on the Battlefield looking and listening for spirits.

Although I have heard a lot of unexplained noises and caught movement from the corner of my eye and have seen what look like figures in the distance, I cannot truly say that I had seen a ghost until May 7, 1997.

When someone tells you what they have seen and no one can change their mind, I know just how they feel. You just know what you saw.

I have friends and family in Gettysburg but, I don't like to impose, so I stay at different campgrounds. They all have little cabins that I adore.

I was staying at one of my favorites. There were Civil War tents next to the cabin that I had rented. They gave the place a quaint look.

In the evening of this particular night in May, my husband, aunt and I were sitting at the picnic table talking. It was growing quite late.

I happened to look over at the tents and standing there was a Union soldier. He looked as if he were standing in a dim spotlight. Our eyes locked. I could not speak or pull my eyes away. I heard nothing my husband and aunt were saying. I saw nothing but this sad yet determined looking man. I saw everything about him, his neat but dirty uniform, his long smooth beard and mustache and his hair curling up around his bummer(hat). He had long fingers and I even saw the symbol on his jacket. It was the three leaf clover. With my knowledge of Civil War history, I knew immediately he was from General Winfield S. Hancock's 2nd corps. It was his eyes, dark brown and so drawing, that I could not pull my own away from.

Suddenly, as quickly as he appeared, he was gone. Then, and only then, did I jump up.

Much to my surprise, my husband and aunt saw nothing. That sent my mind reeling. How could they not have seen him? He was so real. I will never forget him. I still see him in my mind.

When I went to bed that night, I couldn't get the song, "The Battle Hymn of the Republic," out of my head.

Was it wishful thinking? I hope not, I would like to believe this lost soul appeared to me because I feel so strongly for their suffering and the loss of such brave men.

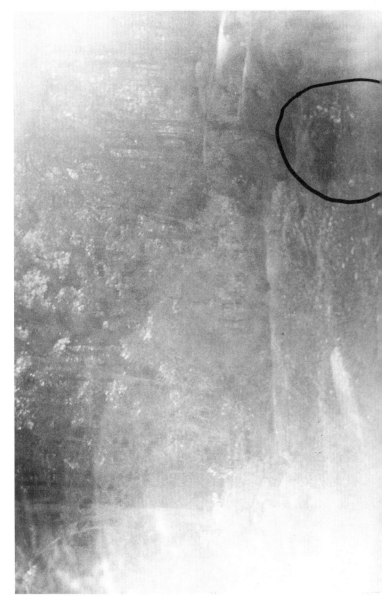

This picture of Devil's Den was taken on a beautiful, sunny day. As you can see, there appears to be legs in the circle that I have drawn around.

My husband and I captured this cloudy form passing by, while staying at one of the campgrounds.

This was sent by Hildred Robinette. Taken at Cavalry Field where Gen. J.E.B. Stuart's men waited and died in the woods. You can see a small puff of smoke. It was a sunny day with no fog and no reason for the smoke. Within the circle to the left there appears to be two Rebel soldiers sitting on a log. On the right there seems to be a wounded Yankee soldier.

HITCHING A RIDE

While walking around Devil's Den one sunny afternoon, I met a beautiful couple from Ohio, Jerome and Alicia Jackson. This was their third trip to Gettysburg. The man, woman and teenage daughter related to me how much they had fallen in love with this place. They also told me that they would never return to East Cavalry Field again.

I explained to them that I was doing research on East Cavalry.

I always have trouble explaining what exactly it is that I am researching. I've sacrificed a good reputation, many times being called insane or had folks be down right sarcastic. "Are you nuts?" was the most famous one. Not all believe, and that's ok. Some do and others are willing to open up, where others are reluctant at first.

I had to pry a little but, when they started their tale, their words flowed like hot fudge down a sundae.

On their second trip to Gettysburg they parked out at East Cavalry Field and decided to get out of the truck and walk around for a while. After their long trip, they needed to stretch their legs.

If you're not on a ghost hunt, being in the park after dark is very relaxing and beautiful. I love to sit at the bottom of Little Round Top when the moon is full and the air is cool and crisp. Sometimes, the frogs are so loud that they drowned out the other night sounds.

The Jacksons walked for a while, then got back into the truck. Their daughter got into the back seat of the truck and opened the back window for some air. With all their windows down, they could feel the breeze gently blowing. They sat there for awhile talking softly and enjoying the night air. Looking into the field to the right, not knowing exactly what drew their attention there, they saw a cloud of fog slowly form into what looked like a group of men in formation.

As they sat quietly and watched the men as they marched back and forth, they were totally mesmerized. Although it had only been minutes, they said it seemed like hours while they watched.

Then, they felt the bed of the truck go down as if someone was climbing inside. Their trance was broken from the field and they swiftly turned to look in the back. Dad however, never turned around. He gazed amazingly through the rear view mirror. When mother and daughter looked in back of the truck, they saw a Confederate soldier sitting patiently. At that moment their truck went down again as if another were getting in.

Both mother and daughter started to scream, while father sat and watched his rear view mirror turn slowly upward. Fearing that his daughter was becoming hysterical, he started the truck. Being frightened himself, he had to make a great effort to control his driving.

They emphasis very strongly that this really happened and all three could not have imagined it.

Apparently, the boys just wanted a ride home to Virginia or whatever southern state they had come from. It was a long walk to Gettysburg.

Maybe the back of a pickup truck looks like a wagon of their time and they wanted a ride. Who's to know?

PULLED BACK IN TIME

I love this story told to me by Arthur and Joan Bivins, a family from Mississippi. They still take the war very seriously. The story they related to me baffles me to this day.

Arthur always felt that he was in the battle between J.E.B. Stuart and George Custer at Cavalry Field. He visited there many times and felt drawn to the place where Fitz Lee fought.

He would just sit and watch out over the horizon, where the fierce battle took place.

On his last trip, while sitting in the car, he felt as though he were hypnotized.

Arthur had his aunt and Joan with him and they both started feeling sick to their stomachs.

As they sat and watched, the tree in front of them began to move away, as if they were being pulled backwards. The women began screaming at him to get them out of there but, he didn't respond.

Finally in desperation, his wife grabbed his arm and began shaking him furiously. He remembers feeling very relaxed. He saw a huge cloud and in that cloud he saw men calling to him. He felt as if he knew them and wanted to be with them.

He fought his way through the thick cloud and he could almost touch them, almost feel them.

Suddenly, he was shaken out of his trance and thrown back into reality. He knows that it wasn't a dream because he was not asleep, but he felt as though he were in another time. He believes that they were his men from the dreadful day on July 3, 1863, calling to him to come back and be with them.

He explained that he always felt as though he had fought as a Rebel officer in Gettysburg. His encounter with his men proved it to him.

He confessed that when he is alone and daydreaming, he feels a strong longing to be with them once again.

EAST CAVALRY FIELD, JULY 3

*"LIKE THE FALLING OF TIMBER-SO
SUDDEN AND VIOLENT- THAT MANY OF
THE HORSES WERE TURNED END OVER
END AND CRUSHED THEIR RIDERS
BENEATH THEM.
THE CLASHING OF SABERS, THE FIRING
OF PISTOLS, THE DEMANDS FOR
SURRENDER, AND CRIES OF THE
COMBATANTS NOW FILLED THE AIR."*

CAPTAIN MILLER 3RD PENN. CAVALRY

THE AMERICAN FLAG

A very good friend of mine, Jimmy Selinski, told me he was going to visit Gettysburg. He often scoffed at my tales of the spirits that roam there. His belief was that, "When you die, you die!"

I believe in resurrection. You are born again and again, until you learn lessons in life that make you a good God fearing person.

I also believe that a soul can be tormented and lost in a time that they can't let go of.

So many soldiers went on, yet so many more did not. They believed so strongly in a cause, they continued to fight a war that was long forgotten.

When Jimmy returned from Gettysburg, I found his story very interesting. He left a diehard nonbeliever and returned with a whole lot of room for doubt.

He explained that while he was at the Peace Light, he parked along Oak Ridge. This is where many of the Confederates were mowed down by the North, when they stood up from the breast works and wiped out line after line of South Carolina's fighting men.

While parked there, Jimmy called out for the Confederates to surrender. Mocking and laughing, he asked them if they needed shoes. While doing so, he waved a small American flag.

Nothing out of the ordinary happened until he started to drive away. He heard a very loud bang, as if someone had thrown a rock at his car.

Once again he proceeded to drive away and once again he heard the same loud bang. He didn't get out of his car to investigate but, for the remainder of his trip he decided not to aggravate the Rebs.

Do they still take slurs of losing seriously?? Well, someone had a good aim that night. It wasn't uncommon for the Rebs to throw rocks if they ran out of bullets, they had to use something. It also didn't surprise me that from that experience he thought differently about the hereafter and about Gettysburg.

Peach Orchard

THE GENERAL

Some of my story tellers prefer to keep their identities confidential, while some tell me that they do not care who knows about them, for they truly believe in what they claim to have seen. That is how my next story teller, Sarah Hattis felt.

After living in Gettysburg for 12 years, she has had many occurrences that simply cannot be explained away. She is the mother of my son's friend. After her divorce, she moved back to New Jersey.

As she told me of the experiences in her home, I felt drawn to her. There was a certain sadness about her. She was alone with three children to raise, and in my eyes, she was very brave. She was so believable that I dwelled on her every word.

She had a run in with a general in her home many times. Living off Route 30 put her in the area that General John Bufford was trying to hold back from General Heath's division, so that the Union could get to the high ground. You might say that her home was right in the thick of things.

Many times, she saw a Confederate general standing in her back yard with his hands on his hips and his legs spread apart in a defiant pose.

She has also smelled the scent of cigar or pipe tobacco drifting in the windows on a soft morning breeze.

After seeing General Barkdale's picture, she thinks it was him that she saw. Barkdale was mortally wounded in the Peach Orchard.

Many nights after the children were asleep, she lay in her bed listening to the sound of men crying out for help or moaning in pain.

It was so unnerving at times, that during the sweltering summer heat, she would close the windows rather than listen to the cries of the dead.

A few times, while sitting at her desk, she thought she smelled sulfur. She knew the smell of gun powder and said that there is no mistaking it.

I believe that this woman could write a book of her own with the many ghostly encounters she has experienced. Her children have also seen soldiers, with rifles in hand, scurrying behind trees, as if dodging enemy fire.

The children have also seen a general many times with his hands on his hips. They have also seen him with his sword held high in the air, as if he were leading a charge.

The family's claim was so believable, mainly because I have never heard a five-year-old child give such an accurate description of a general, unless she has seen one for herself. The child also told me that she could see the sun shine off of his really long knife(sword).

The eight year old boy told me that he could even see that the general had a little bit of gray in his beard.

None of the children felt any fear from the general, they felt as though he liked them and meant them no harm.

If they were out playing, they would call for the general to join them.

Although Sarah is glad that she moved, the children, she claims, miss their general.

UNION GENERAL, JOHN BUFORD

TO

UNION GENERAL, JOHN REYNOLDS

"THE DEVIL'S TO PAY!"

JULY 1, 1863

Confederate guns at East Cavlary Field

YES, . . . THEY STILL ROAM

A male friend of mine, whom I've known for many years, is also very psychic.

Knowing that he is a firm believer in the after life, I asked him to join my daughter and myself on one of our little outings to East Cavalry Field.

After discussing Gettysburg with him, I found out that he was well educated on the Civil War.

Much to my surprise, he knew a great deal about the war and was more than willing to go along.

We were driving through the park and stopped along side the road in front of Gen. George Custer's Monument. It had been raining heavily for a couple days but, we decided to walk up to the monument. While we were walking, I noticed the many puddles about the field. As I looked down at them, they reminded me of blood. I felt cold and sad. I thought of the blood that soaked this ground so many decades before. Seeing the puddles reminded me of the awesome battle fought here. Looking over at my daughter, I saw that she too was looking down at the puddles. I then looked over at my friend. He looked as though he was hypnotized. He gazed out into the field where Custer and J.E.B. Stuart clashed. He seemed to be watching some battle that we couldn't see.

I asked him what he was watching and he proceeded to tell me what I was hoping to hear.

He told me of the torment, the battle between man and beast, the thunder of hooves, the deadly screams of dying men and when it was over, the songs of glory.

He felt as though he was going through the battle over and over again. I was astonished and had no wind with which to speak. We moved onto the southern side of the battlefield.

I watched his face for some kind of hint as to what he was seeing or hearing. His expression was troublesome. "What?", I asked, with a mixture of excitement and fear.

He expressed to me that there was so much pain and hate. It was a slaughterhouse. The soul of a demon roamed these woods and this was not a good place. There was so much animosity and pain here that the demon fed on this hatred that the lost souls of the past had left behind. He said that he heard the cries of a young soldier where he lay burned and dying in the woods calling, "MAMMA, MAMMA!"

He heard yet another crying out for help with his throat slashed from a saber as he lay bleeding to death. There was so much carnage, most of which came from the emotional suffering that all those men had to endure.

Many of them had no shoes to wear, their feet torn and blistered, cut and scraped from the briers and thorns. Their clothes in tatters, they carried around the feeling that their family back home was not in any better condition than they were. With all this upon them, they also had the dark cloud of death and war hovering over their heads.

My daughter was suddenly in tears saying, "No one should be made to suffer the way these men suffered."

If only we could make it right. My friend was very positive that the spirits of both sides were still active . . .

I am so looking forward to our next trip together.

WHISPERED LOW, THE DYING SOLDIER.
PRESSED HER HAND AND FAINTLY
SMILED.
"WAS THAT PITYING FACE HIS
MOTHER'S?"
DID SHE WATCH BESIDE HER CHILD?
EVERY VOICELESS WORD WITH
MEANING, HER WOMAN'S HEART
SUPPLIED.
WITH HER KISS UPON HIS FOREHEAD,
"MOTHER", HE MURMURMED AND DIED.

UNKNOWN

Triangular Field where many men died and many cameras fail to work.

SOMBER FEELINGS

Upon one of my many visits to Gettysburg, I met Dave and Judy Blueher, from Syracuse, New York. During a conversation with the middle-aged couple, I learned that not only had they visited Gettysburg once before, but in fact, during their last visit, Judy had an encounter and a rather horrific experience. Her story, like so many others, will truly amaze you.

Judy's encounter began on a warm summer day in July. During that day, the couple stopped to view one of the many monuments on the battlefield. They were also admiring Triangular Field.

The field gave off an aura of beauty and a sense of fullness, yet seemed peaceful. Judy was captivated by the tall trees that surrounded the field, the purple flowers that grew between the trees and the green grass that covered every inch of dirt.

In front of the field, still standing after so many years, was an old rickety gate. Infatuated by the field, Judy walked slowly toward the old gate. As she approached the gate, a sense of uneasiness fell upon her. She hesitated to go any deeper into the field but, for some unknown reason, Judy continued walking.

Within a matter of minutes, her body was engulfed by a peculiar, bone chilling coldness. Not finding the strength to move, her hands trembling fiercely, her eyes filling with tears, her mind raced to find an answer for what exactly had come over her.

While still standing in Triangle Field, with the wind gently blowing, she recalls sensing a great deal of pain. As if shot or cut by some unseen force, she held back the anger and sadness of something she was not sure of.

Soon Triangle Field had no aura of beauty or fullness, nor was it peaceful. For this woman, on this day, Triangle Field was filled with a sorrowing mist of death.

What exactly was she feeling? Could she have been caught in the middle of a crossfire and shot? Could she feel or sense the death and carnage of the southern boys who died here?

She thinks she did.

This is where Don saw the three Yankee soldiers cross the road at Cemetery Ridge.

THREE WOUNDED YANKS

I decided to do these two stories together because of their similar circumstances. Don Arybola had recently moved to Gettysburg from Bristal Pa. He joined up with the 57th Pennsylvania. He is a devoted re-enactor and looks dashing in uniform.

After meeting Don one summer night, we became good friends. He stops by every now and then to chat. One particular night he stopped by because he needed to talk to me about a sighting he had just had.

He was driving slowly along Cemetery Ridge. The third day of the great battle, this place was where the men fought and died gallantly. There were wounded and dead as far as the eye could see.

Don claimed his mind was on nothing else but the upcoming re-enactment. He explained that although he did believe strange things happened in Gettysburg, he himself had never seen a spirit. He had experienced occurrences such as doors slamming, tapping on the steps or his dog looking down the steps whimpering.

He passed these off as being an old house and didn't think much of it.

As Don casually drove along the ridge, three Yankee soldiers came from nowhere. Their faces were soot smeared and they were battle worn.

At first, he thought they were re-enactors. As he stared in awe, he noticed that the middle soldier had his arms around his two comrades. He recalls that it looked as if they were dragging him along.

One of the soldiers looked back at him with hopelessness. They proceeded to the rear, which would be Taneytown Rd.

They disappeared just as quickly as they had appeared.

Don, a big, strapping young man was overcome with a feeling of desperation. He sat there with tears running down his cheeks. He remembered feeling such compassion for them.

All the suffering they seemed to be going through, and it goes on and on.

He explained to me how this experience would make him a better re-enactor. He is very intent on teaching the history of the Civil War so that their suffering and patriotism will not be in vain.

Pickett's Charge where Barbara saw a ghost playing bag pipes.

BAG PIPES

After moving to Gettysburg, the first couple I was fortunate enough to meet were Barbara and Ron Ogburn.

Barbara does free lance photography. They reside in Littletown, Pa.

They were kind enough to share their first ghostly encounter with me. Barbara and Ron loved to take their evening ride on the battlefield looking for wildlife. There is an abundance of wildlife out there and I enjoy looking for deer and fox which roam freely in the battlefield as well. But, Barbara and Ron were going to get more than wildlife. For you see, their life was about to get wild.

While out riding one night, they were passing the statue of Robert E. Lee. This is where the fearless and undaunted men of the Confederacy marched in perfect formation a mile across an open field under cannon fire from Union forces on Cemetery Ridge; it was a slaughter.

Union forces peered over the stone fence, looking in awe at the proud Rebel troops. No Civil War troops ever attacked in such an open field at this distance before.

As they were struck down like ripe wheat, their lines would close up and onward they came. The men that made it to the stone fence were quickly killed or surrendered. The rest that returned to their lines were shocked at the carnage in front of them.

Their comrades heads, limbs and bodies were blown apart by cannon fire. This attack was known as Pickett's Charge. Over 6,000 men lay dead upon that blood soaked field. Was it any surprise that some of these souls who died so brutally seem to wander the field of their death?

It was one of the sightings on the bloody field that Barbara and Ron witnessed their first encounter.

Hearing bag pipes, they pulled the truck over and listened, deciding to get out and look around to find the source of this lovely music. They walked to the field and saw a man walking all alone. To their surprise, he was playing "Amazing Grace". Ron, having his binoculars along, looked out into the field. To his astonishment, he saw a Scotsman marching slowly across the field. Thinking he was playing a tribute to someone, they proceeded into the battlefield to investigate.

To their amazement, he vanished. "Here one moment, gone the next". I might add that they had never experienced a sighting before nor believed in ghosts. It was the farthest thing from their minds, yet, there he was.

"Explain it!" No one in Gettysburg can.

Barbara has some extraordinary pictures of the paranormal and she and Ron belong to the Adams County Ghost Hunters Club.

So, for you who don't believe, I respect that but, someday or some night you just may see one of the lost souls. Then, you too, may start to wonder. Are there really ghosts? Seeing is believing.

National Cemetery across from Colton.

Herr Tavern.

JOSHUA

The first day of July opened the battle of Gettysburg. General John Buford saw a black cloud gathering over the town of Gettysburg and knew a fight was brewing.

His premonition came true. Checking the ground, Buford understood the strategic significance of the land. Appreciating the value of the high ground, Buford was to hold it for the Union and the fight that was sure to come.

Buford was determined to hold the high ground and pitted his 2,800 horse soldiers against General Henry Heth's 16,000 Confederates. He purposely held them back in order to give the Union time to come up. The fighting to hold the Rebels back was fierce along Herr's Ridge.

The two brigades were quickly forced back. Buford did what he set out to do. The Union flag was up and he held the high ground.

Upon Herr's Ridge sits the historical Herr's Tavern that has many tales of ghostly hauntings.

While dining there one evening, my husband and I struck up a conversation with a very busy waitress. Even though she was the only one working, she found time to divulge two quick tales of ghostly encounters. While my husband, a history buff, wandered around this beautiful dining room full of history, I was enjoying my delicious meal and a story.

She said one night she and a coworker were working late. No one else was there. Suddenly, a large trash can with speed of it's own went sliding across the kitchen floor. This led to Joshua, their resident ghost, who seems to haunt Herr's Tavern. Having a psychic go through the tavern, she found a young Confederate soldier there by the name of Joshua.

He was killed on the first day of battle, for reasons only he and God know. He has taken up residency at Herr's Tavern, playing pranks from time to time, thus keeping the place lively (no pun intended). If you're visiting Gettysburg and looking for a place to dine, try Herr's Tavern. The food is excellent, the service is 1st class and you just may catch a glimpse of this young Confederate soldier, who for some reason, has refused to cross over.

Chamberlain's 20th Maine, back of Little Round Top.

CANNON FIRE

One of my favorite Generals was Joshua Chamberlain. He and the 20th Maine, as others, fought gallantly on Little Round Top against the Alabamians.

After a fierce charge, they captured the Rebs and held Little Round Top.

I took a ride out to the battlefield one Tuesday afternoon in November and parked at the Chamberlain monument. It was a calm day. I was alone, sitting there listening to the music from the movie Gettysburg.

Looking up at the monument and into the barren woods beyond, I couldn't help but think how brave those long ago soldiers were.

It is sad when a life is taken but, it is even sadder when it is taken needlessly. As the music played, I turned it up, opened the windows and yelled out, "This music is for you boys, for your bravery."

Sitting there for ten more minutes, I turned off the radio. I no sooner did that, when I heard a loud explosion. I could feel the jeep vibrate. I'm not sure what it was but, I know it sounded like the bellow of a cannon.

I had hoped they heard me and appreciated the music as I did. I believe that they still roam the battlefield. Too many people have seen them, heard them, and yes, even felt them.

Maybe someday we will find a way to communicate with them so that we may set them to rest, and they can give up the fight they have been fighting for so long.

7th New Jersey Monument.

THE HEADLESS SOUL

With a hardy Yankee cheer, the brave Seventh New Jersey men headed toward the Peach Orchard and certain death.

There before them stood a full line of General Barksdale's Mississippians. The Seventh New Jersey took a terrible beating that day. One hundred and fourteen were killed, wounded and missing. The few that remained struggled to make it to safety. Is there any wonder that there are so many sightings on this hollowed ground?

Folklore has it that one of the Seventh New Jersey boys had been beheaded that bloody day at the Peach Orchard. It is said that he still roams these beautiful fields. There have been sightings of a lonely soldier slowly walking up the Emmitsburg Road, holding onto the long white fence to guide his way. He can't see where he is going, for he had no head.

Perhaps, he is trying to make it to the safety of Cemetery Ridge.

Cemetery Ridge where General Robert E. Lee told his men to aim for the trees.

UNSEEN BOOTS

I met a young man who was investigating the paranormal just as I was and he told me of a couple of occurrences that happened to him while he was recording.

He caught me by surprise; I have not found many people who know about getting some of these ghostly sounds on tape.

One evening, about nine o'clock, he put his recorder up on the Bible at Cemetery Ridge. He returned to his car to sit and wait.

An hour later, he retrieved his recorder and went home to listen to his tape.

He was astonished to hear heavy walking, as if a big man in boots approached. The steps walked right up to his recorder, then stopped. Suddenly, his recorder was shut off. He told me what threw him for a loop was that he was only sitting twenty-five feet away and the whole time he was sitting there, he never saw a soul walking around.

He gave me the privilege of listening to his tape. I heard him place the recorder on the Bible. I also heard the stones crunching under his feet as he walked away. Then, I heard the slight sound of his car door shutting as he got back into the car.

Within a matter of minutes, I heard the sound he so clearly described to me. It was the sound of very heavy footsteps walking toward the recorder. Then there was a sudden snap and the recorder went off.

Now, this young fellow had my undivided attention. He let me listen to a tape from a few days earlier.

I could hear cars passing by, then I heard the sound of a man with a deep voice yelling out his orders. Although I couldn't make out every word, I heard him so clearly.

For a while all was quiet, then again right out of the blue came a moan, some more yelling, then more moaning.

The whole experience sounded as if they were in an echo chamber. It sent chills up and down my spine.

Cemetery Ridge was where the battle of July 3rd took place. It was better known in history as Pickett's Charge. There were over twelve thousand men that lost their lives in the bloody battle. What I heard was not of this time, but of a time in the past. A time when men yelled as they raged into battle.

Officers bellowed their orders and men moaned from their many wounds. I believe that I was hearing the sounds of the battle drifting in on the winds of a time long, long ago.

PICKETT'S CHARGE
JULY 3, 1863

"UP MEN, AND TO YOUR POST! DON'T FORGET TODAY THAT YOU ARE FROM OLD VIRGINIA!"

CONFEDERATE GENERAL, GEORGE PICKETT

Sach's Bridge

THREE WOUNDED REBELS

I always enjoy newcomers to Gettysburg. They are so inquisitive.

While I was out taking pictures on Sachs Bridge, I met Dan Bryson of Riverside, New Jersey.

Sachs Bridge is full of historical information. The Confederate and Union soldiers crossed the bridge to do battle on northern soil. A short walk from the bridge is a Civil War Hospital.

The dead were buried along the bank of Marsh Creek. This is the creek that Sachs Bridge covers.

After the hideous battle ended, 17 miles of General Robert E. Lee's wagon train passed over and near the bridge.

The seriously wounded were carried in the wagons. The less wounded walked, or were helped by their comrades.

After fighting a devastating battle for three long days, many of the Rebel soldiers could barely carry themselves home.

As they struggled to make it back to Virginia, they took hold of the weaker and wounded to help them along.

I spoke to Dan and his friend, John, for about 10 minutes. They explained that they were leaving early the next morning and wanted to see the bridge before leaving.

Dan confessed no interest in the Civil War, while John couldn't get enough of it.

Although I collect ghost stories, I do not give this information freely. I do a little detective work first. If they don't mention it, I find it better to leave it alone, not everyone believes and that's fine. If you see, hear or even smell something unusual, no one can tell you any different. I have had all three encounters.

I proceeded toward the back of the bridge and Dan and John headed for the field. They spotted a deer earlier and went out looking for her.

It was a clear night in October, but it was cold. The moon was almost full so I needed no flashlight.

I heard John say he was going to get his gloves from the car. All of a sudden I heard someone yell, "ahahahahah." Looking back, I saw Dan as he passed me in a frantic run. He didn't stop until he reached the end of the bridge.

He made a complete circle as if confused as to where to go. I approached him cautiously, as I did not know what was wrong with him.

John then came running up, asking what was wrong.

Dan was trying to tell us what he had seen in the field. He was stuttering uncontrollable. If I hadn't been so concerned for him, I'm sure I would have laughed.

Slowly, as he gulped air, he told of his startling encounter with the paranormal. Shaking his head and still gulping for air, he explained his story.

As he looked south into the field, he saw a ball of fog. He remembers thinking how strange that was, for the night was so clear.

He stood mesmerized as three Confederate soldiers appeared from the fog. They were scruffy looking and hollow eyed.

He would stop his story and look as if he were in a trance, as if we were not even there. Then he would shake his head and begin again.

I was dying of anticipation. I felt like I wanted to shake the rest out of him.

Slowly, he continued his horrifying experience.

He explained that there were two soldiers on each end and they were helping a third in the middle who seemed to be wounded.

He watched as one of the men fell down, dragging the wounded soldier with him. As the fallen soldier looked back at him with pitiful eyes, he clearly heard him say, "Help us." Dan said he remembers nothing else until he found himself standing in front of us.

Asking him if he believed in ghosts he exclaimed, "Not until now!"

As in every story I hear, Dan kept saying, "I know what I saw. There were three soldiers in that field."

After calming down he gave me permission to use his story.

I asked him if he were afraid that someone would think he was crazy. His reply was, "I wasn't drinking or I would blame it on that. I have no reason for what I saw, but I know I did see it. I will remember their sad faces until the day I die."

Sach's Bridge

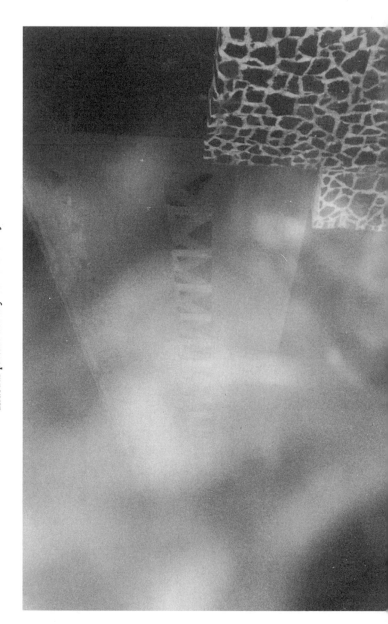

Chris of Hanover Penn., gave me this photo. I was on the bridge one night and met him. He kindly offered me this unusual picture for my book. Thank you Chris.

WHISPER

In May of 1998, Tamara Nickole and her family took a trip to Gettysburg. This is not the first time they had been to Gettysburg. They usually travel from West Monroe, New York once a year on vacation.

They enjoy the many interesting sights there are to be seen and even the ones that choose not to be seen.

During their stay at one of the local campgrounds, they were told about Sacks Bridge and the many experiences that other folks have had while visiting there.

The old bridge was said to have been haunted by a young woman who was decapitated while on her way to a ball. The bridge was also used by Yankee and Rebel soldiers during the Civil War. Sachs Bridge is located along Marsh Creek.

This was not the first time Tamara and her family went looking for ghosts. The first night they were at the bridge, Tamara felt a little uneasy about being there. They decided to leave, only to return the next night. It was around 11:45pm on a chilly Saturday evening. As they got out of the van they glanced at the bridge.

The bridge was red in color with a ledge made of brown stones on each side; they could slightly hear the water that runs below. The sky was dark, not a star to be seen, the wind was somewhat calm.

As they approached the bridge to walk across and see what was on the other side, they were hit with an ungodly cold breeze and the sound of footsteps, as if someone or something was following them.

Needless to say, by the time they got to the other side of the bridge they were not looking forward to the long walk back.

The four of them were so stuck together, they looked like a centipede wearing sneakers. Once Tamara's father untangled himself from the frightened threesome, he made his way back across the bridge.

When they all made it back across, they stood listening and watching. Tamara sat down on the brown stone ledge while the others stood at the entrance way to the bridge.

Tamara was sitting there staring down into the water when someone tapped her on her right shoulder. She looked around and saw nothing out of the ordinary. Thinking it was her father kidding around, she continued to gaze at the water. Suddenly, someone started whispering in her ear. She jumped up, let out a startling scream and ran around in a complete circle, latching onto the back of her fathers jacket. She was shaking so badly her legs felt like they were going to give out at any second.

No one knew what had happened, until Tamara in her quivering voice, tried to explain. In the middle of her explanation a black form of some sort started walking from the very spot where she had just been sitting not seconds ago. It started walking to the other side of the bridge right in front of everyone.

I think that was the last straw for Tamara. She ran, faster than her legs could carry her, back to the van. She was not getting out again until they left that unexplainable place.

THE DEN

Devil's Den, one of most popular sights on the Gettysburg battlefield, with it's masses of boulders and deep crevices, looks rather sinister and a bit mysterious.

The battle for Devil's Den commenced on July 2nd. General Lee wanted the rocks taken and so General John Bell Hood and his Texans were ordered to do so, at a great cost.

After the battle. the scene was horrendous. Dead bodies began to bloat and turn black in the hot sun. Bodies were stuck in the crevices of these huge boulders. Many of them were Sharp Shooters that would pick off the Union soldiers on Little Round Top, directly across from them.

Between Little Round Top and Devil's Den there is a valley. The stream that runs through it is known as Plum Run. It is said that this stream ran under these boulders.The bodies were caught in these crevices, decomposed and fell into the stream. Plum Run was later named "Bloody Run."

The first cameraman witnessed and filmed this costly loss of life. Bodies scattered, some with their eyes wide open and glaring, some smiling, while others were bent and twisted.

The bodies were left to rot in the hot July sun until only a bleached skeleton remained.

One of the cameramen drug a body off the field, put him among the rocks with a rifle in his hand and posed him as a Sharp Shooter so pictures could be taken. This young Rebel was left lying there for four months.

Many of the sightings are of a young, dirty looking, Confederate soldier. He's appeared on numerous occasions.

After visitors take his picture he disappears or they will get home and after having their film developed, he is not to be seen, knowing that he was in their view when they snapped his picture.

At the fireworks this year, a young couple came up to me saying that they heard I wrote ghost stories. They said they had a tape that they wanted me to hear. While visiting Devil's Den Jennifer and John Laurie of Hammonton, New Jersey, put a tape recorder in one of the caves. In a raspy whisper I clearly heard, "Use the flash", then complete silence. Within seconds I heard a whisper, "Flash please", then a low deep moan as if in dreadful suffering. My entire body broke out in goose bumps.

Devil's Den

This did not appear to be a fake. It is not unusual for the dead to speak on tape and they always sound as if they're in an echo chamber. It is clearly different from a human voice.

Maybe this dead Sharp Shooter thought the tape recorder was a camera and was just looking to get another picture taken.

For all of his suffering and disrespect of his dead body, he seems to hold no grudge. He just wants to be in pictures.

Plum Run Bridge at Devil's Den leading to a path in the woods. This is where Joseph felt he was taken prisoner. The unseen foe must have been a Yank as Joseph was dressed as a Conferderate. Both sides died here.

A PAIR OF REBELS

I was introduced to two brothers who are Rebel re-enactors. They were both unwilling participants in a ghostly encounter.

Charles and Joseph Bowser, from Waynesboro, Pa., were kind enough to share their experience with me.

Charles was with his comrades re-enacting Pickett's Charge. It requires and inordinate amount of self control to cross the field. Reliving what the Confederates did is not an easy feat. The vigorous walk to the rock wall under the hot sun is frustrating enough. Then, add the firing and the smoke from the cannons. That takes a lot of determination. Charles made it to the rock wall where the Yanks waited.

Up to this point, it was re-enactment. Then the hand of the supernatural stepped in.

Charles firmly stated that something grabbed his coat, pulled him back and then threw him to the ground. As he lay upon the ground, he could clearly see that no one was around him.

Who could have pushed him?

He was very sure that no human was around.

Describing his experience, he seemed to be sincere and emotional about the whole affair.

Well, hang in there Charles, according to your comrade and foe, this is not uncommon among the re-enactors. Wear that uniform proudly and try to understand that our ghostly soldiers do not quit; realize that you are really not with them.

Joseph's story is interesting because he was not re-enacting. He was merely walking across the bridge at Devil's Den. As he proceeded down the path (while wearing a Rebel uniform I might add), the unexpected happened.

I couldn't help but survey his unconcerned manner, as though it happens all the time. He continued with his story.

While walking the path, a sudden sharp point went into his back. A hollow deep voice said "Keep walking". At about the same time, his girlfriend who was with him, felt hands grab her. She was greatly frightened and ran immediately. Joseph followed suit. He did glance back, yet saw no one. That did not deter them as they reached for the car.

Joseph, being a re-enactor is quite aware of what the spirit world can do.

These are the rocks that were blood soaked and the dead bodies were caught in their deep crevices.

Not many of the re-enactors like talking about their experiences.

Why do they go on fighting that awful war? Those lost spirits, all of their suffering never seems to end. If God, in his wisdom, could possibly show me a way to set them free, I would be eternally grateful.

But, meanwhile they still roam. Fighting hate and suffering...over and over again.

The Peace Light.

THE PEACE LIGHT

The fields of the Forney Farm were sure on the Grim Reapers list of death. As Iverson's brigade of North Carolinians crossed those rich fields, the blood and bodies of these brave soldiers were going to be added to the sod. In a long, straight line the Tar Heels marched to their death. Directly in front of them lay a low rock wall, but unheard and unseen, were union soldiers, laying flat to the ground. Within a wink of the reapers eye the Yanks stood up and took out 500 men. They were being shot down so quickly, they lay dead in a long line.

Their boots perfectly aligned with their comrades, the Tar Heels were buried where they lay, better known today as Iverson's Pits. For years after the battle the farm help refused to work past dusk. They claimed to hear moans of those dead soldiers or feel their presence. Their southern bodies covered by northern soil must surely disturb the souls of these soldiers.

The Peace Light overlooking the fields where the Tar Heels fell and were buried, was dedicated in 1938, by President Franklin Roosevelt. The Peace Light was unveiled from beneath a hugh American flag. It's flame was lighted by a ninety-one year old Union Veteran and a ninety-two year old Confederate Veteran.

There tend to be frequent sightings of the paranormal in that area. Tony Hoover, of Hanover, Pa. related his unnerving tale while sitting on the steps of the Peace Light. He watched a dark shadow slowly walk from the woods to the cannon, then slowly walk back; then repeat itself. After watching this for a few minutes he concluded it was time to call it a night.

One night while shopping at Wal-Mart, I started talking to the sales girl. She went right into her tales from the grave with no encouragement from me. It seems that she too saw a dark form walk from the woods. Upon leaving, her windshield wipers began to go rapidly back and forth. She explained that friends of hers had similar experiences. Their lights would flash and their horns would blow when no one was in the car.

I have heard numerous stories along these lines. Our friendly neighborhood ghosts seems to have a fascination with the automobile.

I sit many a night at the Peace Light hoping to see this shadow who leaves the woods, then slowly returns. So far, he has not shown himself to me but, when he does, I will surely let you know.

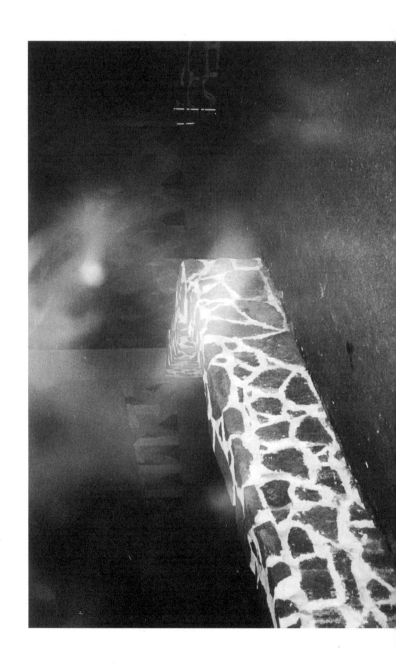

Hildred Robinette sent me this picture of Sack's Bridge. She is from Pitman, New Jersey.

THE FOG

The fog in Gettysburg is eerie. At times it rolls across the fields and farmland. If you are driving, you may hit a large cluster of fog, then driving out of it, it's as clear as a moonlit night. But, there are things in the fog that you would least expect.

One evening, a couple driving toward Devil's Den, saw a pair of bare feet crossing the road. It was only misty out but they could see pure white feet crossing the road in front to them. It is a well-known fact that many of the Rebels had no shoes. They were in the right area. The Rebels fought fiercely to take those rocks. Why only the feet? Could it be that this spirit could not conjure up enough energy to fully form?

On a foggy night in October a couple were out for a ride. They loved the fog. They found it mysterious and exciting. They always went for rides when it became foggy but, this particular night was to become an unexplainable event. They were driving down Black Smith Shop Road. Along this road sits the Sprangler Farm. During the Civil War this farm, as many did, became a hospital. The suffering at this hospital was beyond our comprehension. The doctors worked feverishly to save lives. Many were lost. Arms and legs were amputated and thrown in piles outside the windows to be buried or burned. Men lay on the ground while the maggots ate at their infected wounds. The moans and cries for water and the screams of pain must have left an effect upon this earth that no one understands.

The pain and suffering may have been carried over into the spirit world. It is not uncommon to hear a story of moaning being told among the living.

As the husband and wife approached this farm, that is exactly what they heard . . . a long and low moan. Suddenly a white form dashed out in front of them. The man quickly slammed on the brakes as his wife screamed. They sat in the middle of the road, with the engine running and stared straight ahead in amazement.

The woman explained to me that it looked like a man hunched over as if dodging bullets. Her husband saw the same thing.

It is always helpful when someone else sees the same thing because it's not uncommon to go home and talk yourself out of it by saying, "It may have been my imagination." I, for one, have never heard of two people imagining the same identical ghost.

Spangler Farm Civil War Hospital.

Taney Town Road-Civil War Hospital

*WHAT HAS GONE, TAKES SOMETHING
WITH IT, AND WHEN IT IS OF THE DEAR,
NOTHING CAN FILL THE PLACE.
ALL THE CHANGES, TOUCH THE
BORDERS OF SORROW.*

Major General Joshua Chamberlain

THE ROCKING CHAIR

To my utter enjoyment, I met a female re-enactor with Parcel's Battery. This is her account of what happened.

Amy Thinner, from Waynesboro, Pa., was with the battery in camp, sitting around a warm campfire as a cool breeze rustled through the trees.

She and her comrades noticed two Confederate soldiers going in and out of the food tent. They didn't think too much about it, but there was one re-enactor among them that did believe in ghosts.

After noticing that the tent flap was never untied or opened, he immediately knew what they were dealing with.

Being curious, he yelled to them to come sit by the fire. The two soldiers did not float or glide but merely walked over to the fire.

One sat on the ground across from them. The other preferred to sit in the shadows in an old rocking chair.

He seemed to be content to be concealed in the darkness.

As they watched him slowly rock, they tried to keep their composure.

The first soldier removed his boots and put them next to the fire. The Captain advised him not to put them so close to the fire for they would burn. He then moved them back.

The two scruffy and dirty Rebels never spoke a word. As the participants of this spine chilling encounter watched, the dirty, cold, and hungry Rebels slowly faded away.

Path beyond Devil's Den.

THE DARK MAN

Amy had another encounter with the spirit world. While dressed in southern attire, she decided to walk the path beyond the bridge at Devil's Den. It was just before dusk and a few people were walking around.

She proceeded to walk down the path, when from the corner of her eye she saw movement. She experienced a feeling of pure evil. As she moved forward on the path, a black form darted out in front of her. She could not describe him, only that it was the black form of a man. He went so quickly across her path, she could not identify him.

She related that her only interest was to get out of there. She said she grabbed her hoop, pulled it up and ran like hell, not caring what anyone thought.

We are mere mortals and do not understand the mission these men in the Blue and Gray are still on.

Fitz Lee's Plaque

THE SHADOW

Belle and Norman Astor of Raleigh, North Carolina told me a tale of interest. This was their third trip to Gettysburg. It wasn't customary for them to go on the battlefield at night but, they were leaving in the morning and they wanted to place a flag on Fitz Lee's plaque, which was on the Rebel side on East Cavalry Field.

Having heard the ghost stories of Gettysburg and going on the ghost tours in town, they still weren't convinced that there were such things. Belle said it was a beautiful, clear, moonlit night.

They became extremely nervous after hearing footsteps in the woods behind them. The moon was shining into the woods and it gave an eerie affect to their surroundings. Her husband nudged her and whispered, "I see someone moving around in the woods, it's a dark form!"

As Bell turned to look, she saw an open area in the woods as the bright moon lit up the area. Low and behold, she saw the dark shadow of a man dart across this clearing. As she attempted to explain this to me she became highly nervous. She said she just started running, then realized that the car was in the other direction. Both were very frightened as they got back into the car and took off. They realized they had forgotten to leave the flag. Not wanting to go back, the flag now hangs on the wall of their den.

Belle said for weeks every time she shut her eyes she could still see that dark shadow cross the clearing in the moonlight.

J.E.B. Stuart hid his men in these woods so the Union could not tell how many men he had. Perhaps he forgot one?

7th Michigan, General George Custer, Union side.

OVER AND OVER AGAIN

While shopping in town one sunny afternoon, I met the sweetest elderly lady. I helped her with her packages, as she had more than she could handle. I offered her a ride home and she gladly accepted.

Once we got her packages into the house, she offered me a cup of tea. While in discussion, I told her about the material I was collecting and she related a fabulous story of her own.

Her great-grandfather served with the 88th Pennsylvania and was wounded on Oak Ridge, while confronting Iverson's Brigade. She remembered many stories that were told to her throughout the years, of the sacrifices of many men, and the kindness and caring of the men for one another.

There were hate and bitterness for the enemy but, there was also compassion for each other, no matter what color the uniform.

While she related her story to me I could feel the tears well up in my eyes, thinking of the many men who so needlessly lost their lives.

She explained to me that when her husband was still alive, they used to walk their dog out to Cavalry Field. They were getting on in years and no longer walked out to Oak Ridge because it was too far.

She recalled one evening while they walked past General Custer's Monument, they heard the distinct sound of drums . . . Ta-dum, dum, dum, dum. She heard this many nights over the years.

One summer night, while in their beds, they heard the scream of gallant soldiers drift in on the night breeze. She claims that it was not uncommon to hear the sounds of the battle, a cannon rumble or shots being fired in the still of the night.

Over the years, she has experienced many unnatural occurrences. She has never been afraid because deep down she knows they mean us no harm.

They are just repeating the same thing over and over, lost is a world of war and fear, waiting for it to end. Looking for a light of hope to set their spirits free. In their time, it's still going on, and on, and on . . . never ending.

Mrs. Robinette saw another puff of smoke at the same time she took this snapshot. On the left you can see a man in butternut, holding a rifle. Within the smoke you can also see a group of Rebels on the right side of the smoke.

THE BUTTERNUT SOLDIER

I came across this entrancing tale while talking to friends of my family. These people are intelligent and very creditable, so I was extremely interested.

Grace and Bernie Simpson were taking an evening stroll down Gregg Ave. It was a bit cool outside.

They both got the feeling that something was going to happen. Then Grace mentioned that she had feelings of such dread and despair suddenly came upon her. Bernie said that he had the very same feeling.

They spent many evenings walking or riding their bikes in East Cavalry Field and had never seen or heard anything out of the ordinary. They enjoyed looking for the wildlife. They have seen countless deer, rabbits and once they saw a red fox run across the road.

One fateful evening, they saw more than wildlife and became true believers in the Confederate supernatural.

While they walked toward the Chambliss Brigade's plaques and cannons they saw a soldier laying in the road with his arms stretched out, holding his rifle as if he had the enemy within his sights.

They could see him so clearly. He was wearing a butternut uniform and a battered brimmed, slouched hat. Then, as if an unseen hand had pulled a curtain closed, he was gone.

Not certain what they had seen and thinking it was one of the re-enactors, they proceeded down the road.

By this time night had fallen and Bernie had pulled out his flashlight, which he carried on all of their walks.

All of a sudden, that same feeling of dread came upon them again. They felt as though they should run, but they didn't know from what.

When they reached the corner of Cavalry Field, where Fitz. Lee's men set up for their fierce battle against General George Custer, they heard an ungodly and terrifying scream.

They stood frozen. Then they slowly turned to see the same soldier standing not five yards behind them.

As Bernie's flashlight passed across his face, they could see the fierce look of hate upon him. As they looked at each other with total amazement, the soldier once again slowly vanished.

Still panic stricken, they walked slowly back to the corner, as they heard the scream again.

This was the nudge they needed. Instead of finishing their walk, they decided to run the rest of the way home.

Evidently, this southern soldier didn't want any Yanks walking on his turf.

A RE-ENACTOR??

One intriguing story told to me was of a spirit who enjoyed having his picture taken.

One sunny afternoon while filming at Triangle Field, I met a couple. The gentleman was a native Indian who refused to go to Cavalry Field. He said that he had no respect for "Yellow Hair," better known as General George Custer.

We walked through the field together just to see if my camcorder would record after hearing that sometimes equipment would not work here.

They proceeded to tell me that one day when they had their children at Devil's Den, they saw a Rebel soldier. Thinking he was one of the re-enactors, the children asked him if he would pose for a picture with them. Very kindly the man obliged.

After getting the film developed, only the children were in the picture.

There was a story written about a dead soldier who was dragged four hundred feet out of the field in which he was shot down, propped up and made to look like a Sharp Shooter.

The poor boy's body was only used to make an exciting picture. After the picture was taken, the boy's remains were left in the Sharp Shooter's den to rot in the sun for four months. When he was finally discovered, only his skeleton remained.

Someone's son, brother or husband's body was used and abused, yet he returns. Not as a mean spirit, but as one who is willing to have his picture taken with small children.

These hauntings are like the spirit telling us that he forgives and doesn't mind having his picture taken, and doesn't mind being around humans.

If the tormented soul can return to show their suffering, there hurt and their hate, why not their forgiveness? I might add, that sunny afternoon in October, I had no problem taping in Triangle Field.

General George Custer, 7th Michigan, Union side.

GENERAL G. CUSTER;

IT WAS THE FIRST TIME I HAD EVER
HEARD HIS NAME, BUT AFTERWARD, I
HAD OCCASION TO BECOME VERY
FAMILIAR WITH IT.

Unknown Conferderate Soldier

This was taken by me. I was at the woods across from the plaque of Gen. Fitz Lee. I took this picture to Karyol Kirkpatrick, a renowned physic, and asked her opinion. She explained how spirits use the trees to help them form and said the picture was the best paranormal picture she had ever seen. I didn't see the soldier on the left until she pointed it out to me.

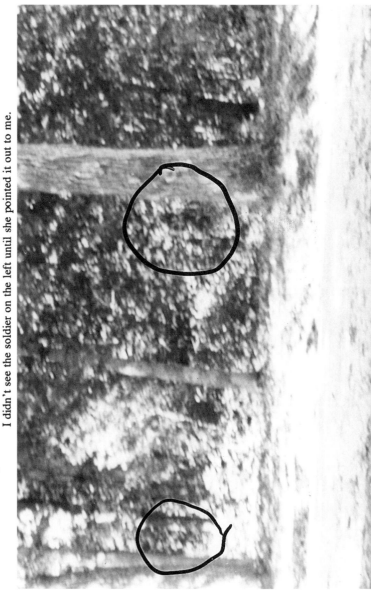

THE STATUE

Willie Allen is a no nonsense kind of guy. He reminds me of a football player. He told me he was a guidance counselor for a high school in Canada.

We were both admiring General Winfield S. Hancock's monument on Cemetery Hill, when he asked me where he could buy a tape on ghosts in Gettysburg. I asked him if he were a believer in ghosts and he exclaimed, "I am now." "Why?", I asked innocently.

"Well," he said, "last evening I was at East Cavalry Field. I parked and decided to walk the road from the Rebel side to General George Custer's monument. It was dark by the time I reached the car. I felt so uneasy while I was walking. I felt as if someone was watching me. Looking around, I knew I was alone. You know what I mean?"

He didn't know what I have heard and seen previously.

He continued to tell of his adventure. As he reached the car he heard men mumbling. Although he saw no one he was sure someone was around him; he felt as though someone was watching his every move. He was spooked, but thought it was because of the darkness. As he started to unlock his car door, the wind started picking up and sounded like it was whispering through the trees. He also felt a bitter chill. The feeling of wanting to run came into his mind. He got into his car and left as quickly as he could.

After leaving the area he was reluctant to look back, but he did. There, standing with his leg slightly bent, stood a gray soldier with his rifle facing the woods he had just come out of.

He explained that with the moonlight shining down on him, he looked gray in color. So proud and stiff . . . like a statue. Willie turned away and headed for his motel. He stayed awake the entire night. By daybreak he headed back to the field. Looking for an explanation, he checked the hill where the phantom soldier stood. There were no trees or stumps that resembled a man. He left dazed, for he never believed in ghosts. It was the furthest thing from his mind. He said he intends to find an explanation for his encounter because, there has to be a reason for it. Well Mr. Allen, when you do, please let me know because I've been looking for it all my life.

Devil's Den.

A SHORT RIDE

I was out visiting an area where there seems to be quite a bit of paranormal behavior.

While there, I met Jim Baker from a small town outside of Gettysburg.

He commented that his neighbor had an encounter, or rather his horse did, while out riding one evening on the battlefield. A calm and gentle mare, which he never had a problem with, all of a sudden reared, her eyes frightened and starring, suddenly dropped over on her back, hitting the ground so hard that the saddle horn left a dent in the dirt. The rider managed to jump off just in time, not knowing what frightened his horse but, remembering a few stories of ghostly encounters with animals, chalked it up to his horse seeing something he could not.

I recall hearing many tales of animals acting strangely on the battlefield.

One resident often walked his dog on the battlefield. He remained calm until they reached one particular monument. Within sight of this spot he began to whine and pull away, not wanting to go near that spot. Once he was dragged past the monument, he seemed to be fine. This reminds me of another dog story.

A couple visiting Gettysburg brought along their pet dog "Alfe". They walked from Little Round Top to Devil's Den. Alfe was fine until they reached the large boulders and crevices of the Den. Upon reaching the large rocks he began pulling on his leash and growling. As his master moved closer to one particular cave in the rocks he would not budge but, proceeded to stare and growl. As they moved closer he began to whine and tried to run away. They were truly frightened and decided to leave. As soon as they were on the road, Alfe went back to being himself again.

But still, he had to glance back to make sure that what he had seen remained in the cave.

It is often said that children and animals, with their innocent minds, can see what we can't, because our non believing minds have so much doubt. Can it be that we clearly can not see what the innocent can? Then, when we do finally see, do we still find it hard to believe?

EAST CAVALRY FIELD

LEADING HIS MEN,

THE 7TH MICHIGAN,

GENERAL GEORGE CUSTER RAISED HIS

SWORD AND SHOUTED,

"COME ON YOU WOLVERINES!"

THE LANTERNS

One of my cousins who was raised in Gettysburg, later moved to Harrisburg to teach 6th grade. She recounted this story over the phone. I was living in New Jersey at the time and had made the phone call so, you could say this was one of my most expensive interviews.

She was a teenager at the time, about 15. She and her girlfriends bet one another that they would not be afraid to walk through East Calvary Field at night. The three girls started their long, dark walk. Familiar with the General Custer Monument, they decided to sit there and rest for a while before continuing on. They weren't there very long before they smelled cigar smoke. Asking each other if they all smelled the same thing, all agreed that it was the scent of a cigar. They knew that a great many of the Generals smoked cigars and they kiddingly said they should be honored to have a General sitting with them. They all laughed at the joke. They heard a lot of ghost stories when they were little but, they took no stock in them, they were just stories. The three girls were more worried about running into a skunk or a fox.

They continued their walk with only one dim flashlight in hand and the light of the full moon, which lit up the road. Also, fearing that a Park Ranger would ride up, they kept the light off as much as possible.

It was after 11:00pm and being in the park that late would surely mean their parents picking them up at the Ranger Station.

If that were to happen, they would be grounded for quite some time. They told their parents that they were at each others houses. If they were caught, that would mean double trouble; not only had they lied, but being in the park after 10:00pm was forbidden.

This was early October, it was chilly. They all had jackets on but, the cold seemed to go right through them. The night was even eerier due to the dense fog that rolled across the fields.

They heard a crackling and rustling in the cornfield. Thinking that it was a deer did not slow the beat of their hearts. As they quickened their pace, they couldn't decide if they should turn back or continue on. They had just come across the bend in the road and straight ahead were the cannons of the Confederates. They walked to this point with quick steps and suddenly slowed. They saw two lights coming toward them and dashed as fast as they could toward the cornfield. They weren't fearing the noise they heard earlier; after all, an animal would be better than the Park Ranger. Looking out between the dried up corn stalks, they waited for the car to pass . . . But there was no car.

Cautiously, they stepped out of the corn.

Bewildered, they found themselves on the road once again. They neither saw nor heard the car pass. But what were the two lights that came toward them? Then, again they saw the lights. This time they were not together as a car's headlights would be, but seemingly floating in midair on two different sides of the road, as if being carried by some unseen hand. While standing there watching this mystifying event, they began to tremble all over. Then the lights vanished as quickly as they appeared. Not sure if they should go on or go back, they stood there puzzled. It was only a short run before they would be out of the park. It took enormous effort, but they went on. Feeling the chill of the night (or was it?), they wanted to get out of the park and return home to get warm. At the corner of the park, they only had to turn left and be out, but something unexplained made them look back. Just this sudden urgency to see what was behind them. Looking back, against their better judgment, they saw, once again, the mysterious lights floating softly to and fro. They were going through the tip of the woods and back out again. They could not see what carried the lights, either the fog was too thick or the carriers were invisible to them.

Their young minds told them what they were seeing. They were looking at some kind of pattern from the past, when the soldiers would carry their lanterns through the fields at night looking for their dead or wounded. As they stood watching these wandering lights, the heavy smell of cigar smoke hit them again. They could not take another moment, they turned and ran as fast as they could run. Running until their little lungs could not suck another breath of air, they slowed but never stopped.

To this day, many years later, my cousin has not been back to East Cavalry Field. No one could ever convince my her that she did not see the lights that night. She believes that she saw the lanterns of the long ago dead. Maybe a General sent his men out looking for the wounded and to collect the dead and while he awaited their return, he smoked his cigar.

THE GHOSTLY BRIGADE

The Rangers that patrol our battlefields were told not to discuss the supernatural with the visitors. They are polite and courteous but, will not talk about ghosts!

Although there are many that have not seen a spirit, there are many that have.

Like the re-enactors, they have more opportunities to see them. Being a re-enactor bonds them to the spirit world. They identify with the uniforms, feeling that they are in their time. They seem to materialize more often.

Many re-enactors relate to me their stories from all the battlefields.

For those of you inclined to think Gettysburg is the only haunted battlefield, I would suggest you talk to some of the locals of Petersburg, Vicksburg and Shiloh; you will be surprised to find that there too, lost and lonely souls still roam.

It is understandable that while the Rangers patrol the park night and day, they have some unusual encounters.

Not all Rangers will discuss their sightings with you but, I found one that related a heart stopping episode. I hope you understand why his name is kept confidential.

It was a clear night as an abundance of stars twinkled from the heavens.

The Ranger had heard many stories about Sack's Bridge and on this captivating night he decided to take a ride to the bridge. He parked facing the bridge, got out and advanced toward the center of the bridge. He became considerably concerned as it was comparatively quiet, yet he felt an overwhelming excitement.

Looking forward to the other end of the bridge, he felt the whole atmosphere change. He felt confined. He could not move a muscle. Suddenly feeling vibrations under his feet and looking diagonally across from him, he watched a large patch of fog form.

He went on to say that one minute the fog was swirling, then began to form into a man. As he stood rooted to his spot he could see a whole brigade of soldiers marching toward him.

He stood there gazing at them with keen curiosity. His senses finally kicked in and he made an about face and ran to his car. Anxious to get out of there, he started fishing around in his pocket for his keys and upon finding them, he heard a tremendous noise.

Refusing to look back and taking precaution to lock his doors, he was out of there in seconds. To him it seemed like hours, yet, he had only been there ten minutes. Needless to say he will never go to Sack's Bridge again.

After he went home and relaxed, he went over it in his mind. No matter how hard he tried to explain it, "He could not." He knows he saw a Rebel brigade crossing the bridge.

Are they oblivious to us? Are they still doing what they did 135 years ago? It certainly seems that way.

SACK'S BRIDGE

The red covered bridge is another hot spot for ghostly encounters. Right off Millerstown Road, the bridge crosses the Marsh Creek.

The retreat of the Confederate army crossed this bridge with their wagons full of wounded and dying soldiers. Because they were being persuaded by the Union army they had no time to give the dead a proper burial. They surely could not take them with them in the July heat, so they were buried along the road as they made their way back to the Potomac.

Some are believed to lay beneath the sod around the bridge. Considering the stories told to me by numerous people, this may very well be so.

There are countless encounters with these deceased Rebels, so I shall start with my favorite.

Tony Hoover, who gave me the story of the Peace Light, also related his tale of the bridge.

Tony, who was born and raised in Nanticoke, Pa., now lives in Hanover, Pa., just outside of Gettysburg, where he has lived for the past three years.

I find Tony to be naive about the afterlife and a very quiet, easy going and honest young man who has made a complete turnaround in his life.

I did not understand why he was seeing and hearing things that were not normal. He did not believe in ghosts, yet he was seeing and hearing them. After speaking with a spiritualist, by the name of Hildred Robinette, he felt he understood more about himself. Hildred lives in Pitman, New Jersey and is in Gettysburg at least twice a month. I have spoken to a few people she has done readings for and they say she is very accurate. She has also contributed some pictures for this book.

Besides seeing the soldier at the Peace Light, Tony has seen a black form in the woods by the bridge. There is a wheel chair ramp leading to the bridge where Tony has observed a dark form arrogantly watching him. He sees no features, only the form of a man with his arms folded across his chest. There is a metal railing going up the ramp. When Tony walks by, the railing bangs vociferously. This led to his talk with Hildred. He thought he might have been a Rebel soldier in his past life but, he was not feeling right about it. His ancestors were Union and this left him confused. Hildred said he was a Union soldier in a past life and the reason he is seeing these Rebels is because they resent him.

"They know he's a Yankee and they don't want him around." After learning this, he is diligently studying the Civil War and is saving his money for his Yankee uniform. Tony intends to become a Union re-enactor.

Now when he sits at the bridge at night, he greets his enemy with a cheery, "Hello, is Tennessee here?"

The railing proceeds to bang. Although I have not seen any Rebels, I heard the railing tap in response to Tony's questions. This has left me baffled. I suppose this is better left between Tony and Johnny Reb.

Sach's Bridge.

Tony Hoover.

AFTER THE BATTLE OF GETTYSBURG

*IN 1863, WITH POMP AND MIGHTY
SWELL, ME AND JEFF'S CONFEDERACY
WENT FORTH TO SACK PHIL-DEL.
THE YANKEES, THEY GOT ORDERS
AND GIV US HELL AND WE
SKEDDADDLED BACK AGAIN, AND
DIDN'T SACK PHIL-DEL.*

Wheat Field.

HE MARCHED ALONE

This story came to me from a lovely lady, Jodie Friedel. Jodie used to live outside of Gettysburg many years ago. She is all too familiar with the many ghost stories that have come about over the years. You see, Jodie is also a believer in the spirit world.

As we exchanged conversation, I shared with her some of my stories that I had heard or collected over the years. In return, she shared with me some of her own. Hers was not one that she heard or collected, but one that she had experienced herself.

Over the years, she has had encounters but, never has she experienced any on the battlefield, until the day of October 3rd.

Jodie had spent the day touring the museums along Steinwehr Ave. with her grandson. From there, she drove over to Taneytown Road to view the many monuments in the National Cemetery.

After the cemetery, she decided to take a drive through the "Famous Battlefield".

She veiled Little Round Top and then went over to Devil's Den. From there she headed over to the Wheatfield.

As she sat and observed the Wheatfield, she recalls thinking to herself, the Wheatfield, the horrible Wheatfield, where so many soldiers lay on blood soaked soil. Their poor lifeless bodies scattered in a sea of blue, as far as the eye could see. The dead lie piled in heaps. The wounded were either awaiting death or seeking shelter from the continuous shells hovering over their helpless bodies.

As nightfall began to settle over the battlefield, Jodie felt that it was time to leave. She took one last look at the now quiet Wheatfield. The stillness was quite comforting. The trees had fully grown over the years and the grass, once green, then red, now green again. The land once covered with the battle of many men, was now calm.

While glancing around, she thought that she had seen movement off in the distance. She continued to watch what she thought was a small animal. From the tall of the trees, a white cloud began to form. As it moved across the Wheatfield, it began to take the shape of what looked to be a soldier.

Remembering every detail so clearly, she recalls how this Yank marched with a slow strut, his head hung low. His face expressed no emotion. His jacket swayed with every step that he took. His pants were tucked neatly into his long boots and his rifle was in hand. As he continued to march in a slow steady pace across the Wheatfield, he began to fade away.

Jodie, totally baffled by what she had just witnessed, her heart pounding, her body chilled, kept her eyes set on the field, awaiting the soldiers return. When he did not return, she knew it was time to go.

Looking over at her grandson sitting next to her, she knew that he did not see what she had just seen.

Where was this soldier marching to? Was he in fact alone? If so, where was the rest of the regiment? Were they all dead, yet not dead? Only they know for sure.

THE CAMPGROUND GHOST

I go to Gettysburg three time a week, almost every week.

On one particular trip, I decided to stay at a campground. It has the cutest little cabins that sit among the pine and oak trees. It is also a hop, skip and a jump from General Ewell's Headquarters.

Knowing that his men camped all over the area, I thought this was a grand place to investigate some history . . . or some sightings.

I have found that campers are really fascinating people. They are warm and friendly, with an abundance of stories to tell. I, with pencil in hand, was all ears.

One very convincing gentleman, Wayne Boyte from Vermont, told me of an experience he had around four o'clock in the morning.

Wayne was sitting at his campfire; he could not sleep. As he turned around and looked down the road, he saw a beautiful woman walking along the road in a long white flowing night gown.

He said that she seemed to glow. He could see her blond curly hair blowing in the night breeze, yet he felt no breeze, only a cold chill.

The closer she came to him, the more she faded away. He could not pull his eyes away from her. He said she just faded away. His first thought was, I just saw a beautiful ghost. His second thought was, where did she go?

He sits by his campfire many nights waiting for her to return and when she does, he intends to be there.

Drummer Boy Campground Road where Wayne Boyte saw a lady in white.

NIGHT RIDER

This story came to me from a family that lived on Low Dutch Road.
General Gregg followed General Custer to Baltimore Pike, then placed
Colonel John McIntosh's brigade and Captain Alanson Randal's horse
artillery a half mile south to Hanover and Low Dutch Roads. Considering
the amount of action in that area, I wasn't a bit surprised to hear of this
haunting.

It was a moonless night and the man of the house was having a hard time
sleeping, so he decided to go to the kitchen for some warm milk.

As he stood looking out the kitchen window he saw a ragged old man
sneaking around the backyard, using the trees to cover him. Thinking it was
a prowler, he switched on the porch light and opened the back door.

He looked out the door and saw a southern soldier standing by a tree. In an
instant the soldier was gone.

Many nights they would hear doors slamming in the house. After a
thorough check of everything, they found nothing out of the ordinary. Some
nights they were awakened by the thunderous sound of horses passing
invisibly by in the night.

They would jump out of bed to look out the window, though they knew
they would see nothing.

The passers by seemed to be headed for Cavalry Field on a mission.

One night in particular, the woman was awakened by heavy footsteps
coming down the hall.

Thinking it was her husband returning from his bowling night out, she
rose to greet him.

When she pulled open the bedroom door, before her stood a Union soldier.

He stood there, grimly staring across the room as if something had his
interest, and in an instant he was gone.

The thing that unnerved them the most was that one night before they went
to bed, they went to check on their baby. When they entered the
doorway, there stood a Union soldier, with dark hair and a short bushy beard,
just standing over the crib watching the little one as she slept innocently.

They were very adamant about everything they told me.

I find it hard not to believe them. It wasn't long after that they packed up and moved to the city.

Had this soldier missed his own child that he could no longer see? So many soldiers had to leave their wives and children behind, never to see them again.

Was he somehow reliving the torture of a lost family taken from him so brutally?

What about the galloping horses through the night? Where were they headed? Were they on their way to meet J.E.B. Stuart on the battlefield?

Do they still ride the same ride? Do they still fight the same fight? Are their spirits so tormented that they have to suffer this same carnage over and over again, even in the afterlife?

THE PLAYFUL SPIRIT

While in Gettysburg an elderly couple and their grandchildren were staying at a motel. This motel was built on the battlefield many, many years after the famous battle.

This particular motel was within walking distance to the National Cemetery.

After spending all day touring the battlefield, they headed back to the motel to rest their aching feet.

Too tired to go out to dinner, granddad and the two girls decided to pick up and bring back takeout food.

Grandma decided to lie down and take a nap. As she started to drift off to sleep, the television snapped on. Jumping up, dazed and confused, she fumbled for the remote thinking she must have left it on the bed and somehow hit the power button. She found it on the night stand.

Her family returned and she put it out of her mind and enjoyed her dinner.

The room was a bit stuffy so they decided to turn the air conditioner on. It was early June and the room was very sultry.

The air ran for about 10 minutes and then shut off. Not finding any logical reason for this occurrence, they turned it back on.

It had been an exhausting day and they decided to turn in early. Just then, the telephone rang. The granddaughter answered it but, there was no one on the other end, so she hung up.

Thinking that someone had misdialed, she turned away. The phone rang again. It had only rung twice when she picked up the receiver and said hello. There was still no one on the other end. At that moment, the air conditioner went off. It had been running for the past two hours without any problems.

Granddad turned it back on again and this time it stayed on . . . for now.

Still, they thought nothing of these occurrences.

Later that night, they were all awakened suddenly by the sounds of men yelling, drums pounding and bugles blowing. After jumping up and snapping on the lights, all the sounds were gone.

They sat up most of that night going over what they had experienced, then finally fell into an onerous sleep.

When they woke the next morning, all was forgotten. Off they went to enjoy the rest of their vacation.

That afternoon, grandma took one of the girls back to the room because she was feeling ill and exhausted from the heat.

While the child was napping, grandma stood at the window waiting for the return of the others. As she stood there, the closet door swung open and hit her on the butt.

Yelling out in surprise, she turned to ask the child why she hit her with the door. In a sleepy voice the child asked what she was talking about. Realizing that just a moment ago the child was fast asleep, she could not have gotten out of bed and opened the door without her knowledge.

Then in the same instance, she remembered the night before and a cold chill ran up her spine.

Looking about the room nervously, half expecting someone to be looking back, she noticed her jacket that was hanging on the rack.

Slowly it began to sway back and forth as if some unseen being had just walked by. As if that wasn't enough, the air conditioner went off and the television came on.

Need I say this cut their vacation short??

That evening when granddad came back, they packed up and headed to New York.

They will never admit that it was a spirit. They tried to convince themselves that it was a draft or an electrical problem, and just a wrong number.

But, let's face it, we're talking about Gettysburg here, known to be the most haunted place in the world.

This motel sat right on the battlefield. Maybe there was a lingering soldier who couldn't leave the past behind him.

Perhaps he decided to spend eternity having a little bit of fun with the guests who stay here.

The Colton Motel across from the National Cemetery.

Union side of Cavalry Field, Custer's 7th Michigan. This is where the young man feels he died.

REINCARNATION

I have spoken to many people who feel as though they are drawn back to the battlefield, because they have a very strong feeling that they lived and died during the Civil War in a past life.

One saga that was told to me by a sweet young man, has never left my mind. He was teased as a child for relating the stories about his dreams of being killed in the Civil War, during the battle of Gettysburg.

I have been told many stories of men and women who claim that they believe they lived during this era but, none were as intense as this one.

This young man told me of his first encounter with the realization of his death at Cavalry Field.

As he stood looking out at what is now a cornfield, the whole scene changed, as if he were watching a movie. Like an instant replay, he saw his death pass before his eyes. It was the very same scene that he saw in his dreams as a child.

He was a young man in the 7th Michigan Cavalry, serving under General George Custer. He was proud to be in the Cavalry and to fight for the Union. He was young and he felt as though death could not touch him.

As they started their great charge across the field to meet their foe, J.E.B. Stuart, on that dreadful day of July 3rd, he was filled with power and confidence as he clashed with the Confederates. His horse was shot out from under him. As he withdrew himself from the ground, he was slashed across the face by his enemy's sword. As he fell, he was blinded by his own blood. He could feel it's warmth as it oozed down his face and moistened the soil beneath him. As he wiped the blood from his eyes, a horse came crashing down on top of him. As he lay there crushed and dying, he thought of his mother and father, and how broken hearted and lost they would be without him.

The last thing in that life he remembered seeing was a beautiful woman standing in a white light, telling him to follow her.

He claims that his remains lay in the National Cemetery in Gettysburg. He told me his name and where the stone is, but asked that I not reveal it.

Perhaps that is better for him.

I could see the pain and anguish this man was feeling as he told his story. I feel he believes everything he told me and I believe him as well. This year he will celebrate his birthday on July 3rd. He was born in the year 1963. The date of his death in his previous life was July 3rd, 1863.

Unbelievable?? Not to me. There are so many wonders in life, perhaps we are not supposed to understand them all.

TWO MORE REBELS

My aunt, Ethel Meredith, went to Gettysburg to visit her sister Isabel. Her daughter, Nancy, talked her mother and Aunt Isabel into walking out to Cavalry Field. She recounted the tale to me.

While walking along Gregg Avenue, the early spring evening was calm and cool. When they stopped along the way at the New Jersey Monument to rest, they heard the unmistakable sound of men's voices, talking quietly.

Looking about and seeing no one, they chalked it up to voices being carried from the nearby farm.

They continued their walk to the other side of the field. This was the place where the Confederates camped, thinking they were going to flank the rear of the Federals. They were not expecting to run into General Gregg and General Custer. There was a hot battle in the field and around Rummel Farm. The Confederates set up medical tents in the open field.

As the three approached this area, Nancy stopped dead in her tracks and all three stared in awe. There, beside a cannon, stood two Rebel soldiers as if they were manning the cannons that have been silent for over a hundred years.

As quickly as they saw them, the soldiers vanished. They have no doubt in their minds what they saw. It was so clear to them that they could even describe their height and hair color.

They had to decide which way to go; past the two Rebs or back the other way, toward the mysterious voices. Unless they could fly, they needed to make up their minds quickly. It was growing dark and under no circumstances did they want to be out on the battlefield after dark.

They chose to go back the way they had come. It was easier to convince themselves that the voices were coming from someone's farm.

GETTYSBURG
JULY 2, 1863

*THE HOUR WAS ONE OF HORROR. AMID
INCESSANT MUSKETRY AND THE GLARE
OF BURSTING SHELL, MAKING THE
DARKNESS INTERMITTANT, ADDING
AWFULNESS TO THE SCENE.
THE HOARSE SHOUTS OF FRIENDS AND
FOE, PITEOUS CRIES OF THE WOUNDED
AND DYING.
ONE COULD WELL IMAGINE THAT,
"WAR IS HELL!"*

THE FOOT FETISH

This story came to me from one of the college students. The only name given was Becky.

It was a Saturday night. After persistent studying all week, Becky and her boyfriend were looking forward to a relaxing weekend.

She didn't remember who suggested that they go to Cavalry Field but, it was quiet and they could be alone. Sitting there in her stocking feet, she had a feeling of foreboding.

Suddenly, her date exclaimed, "What was that?" He said he had seen a white mist or form of some kind pass in front of the car. After minutes of staring into the darkness, they decided that it was nothing. They proceeded to make out. They heard a sound, like two cannons going off. Looking up simultaneously, they saw a white form pass in front of the car.

Not sure what they were seeing, they both sat quietly staring out into the darkness.

All of a sudden, Becky started screaming bloody murder. Her date reacted quickly, starting the car and taking off at a high rate of speed.

He didn't know why he had taken off so quickly, nor why his date was screaming.

He only knew he had such a feeling of dread that he had to get out of there.

He didn't stop until they reached the parking lot of the college and then he asked her why she began to scream so.

Becky, under protest, began to explain. She felt something on her foot. Thinking it was something on the floor, she moved her feet up onto the seat. Once again, she felt something rub her foot, ever so lightly. She rubbed her feet together but, in a matter of minutes she felt it again.

This time it was a firmer rub and she could feel the deathly cold through her socks. That was about all she could take.

When she asked him why he had taken off so abruptly, he stated that he had such a feeling of evil that he felt he had to get away.

After doing some research at Cavalry Field they discovered that in the same

location where they were parked, the southerners had their field hospital set up.
This is where the Rebs kept their wounded and dying. Where their limbs were severed, their bodies buried and where they were beaten and slain in vast numbers.

Did they leave behind their hate for the Yank, the distress of their situation, their rage??

Their bellies howled with the pangs of hunger, their tongues were always dry from thirst. Their clothes were torn and dirty. They had no shoes for their feet that had to march across thorns and brambles.

If ever a soul was in torment, theirs were. Are their souls still roaming? And what of the caressing?

Had a soul been that lonely, that he had to once again feel the soft skin of a woman?

Taken on Confederate Avenue. You can plainly see a soldier kneeling in the road.

2nd Civil War Hospital. Taneytown Road.

THE 7th NEW JERSEY

Barbara Winchester of Lubbock, Texas, overheard a conversation I was having about the spirit world.

The young man that I was talking to adamantly disbelieved in any form of the paranormal.

I patiently listened to his point of view, yet, he cut off every explanation that I tried to give. This is one reason why I try not to debate this subject. You either believe, or you don't and I prefer to leave it at that.

Barbara, who was standing just above us, did believe. She was about ready to tell the tale of her personal encounter. As she spoke, she became very excited.

Barbara is the mother of two teenage boys. She is a career woman and is devoted to her family and her job. She is intelligent and an "up front" kind of person. She had my undivided attention.

It was dusk at the Peach Orchard when Barbara and her son Bobby were sitting quietly in the car. They had been sitting there for the last two nights watching the deer out by the Rose Farm.

Barbara said she kept hearing someone crying. The two quickly got out of the car. They proceeded to look for the person that appeared to be in pain.

Hearing the sound again, it seemed to be coming from the Bullet Monument, so they headed for the field. They suddenly stopped dead in their tracks. There, laying upon the ground, was a bloody and torn Yankee soldier.

He was crawling and reaching out as if for some other unseen soul.

Barbara explained that the form looked like heat waves passing over him or like looking into old fashioned glass that distorted his form.

She said it seemed like hours but, only minutes had passed. They stood in shock as he slowly evaporated.

Barbara said the effect this young soldier had on her was devastating.

"He was so young", she repeated over and over again, "just like a child."

I followed as she led me to the spot that she had her sighting. It was about 10 feet from the 7th New Jersey Monument.

General Sickels led New Jersey to their death after he moved his line forward, against orders. This led to the death of many men of the 3rd corps.

Had Barbara and her son caught a glimpse of the past?

I surely hope so. We must never forget our sins of the past, so we may never repeat them.

Barbara now comes to Gettysburg for every vacation.

She and Bobby sit at the Peach Orchard. They are not looking for the abundance of deer that roam in the park, they are hoping to see, once again, the young man who's face haunts them.

General Robert E. Lee overlooking the field they call Pickett's Charge.

East Cavalry Field.

ORBS

For those of you who do not know what an orb is I shall try to explain. It is a sphere that is transparent in the world of the paranormal. It is believed that these orbs or sphere's are ghostly forms that will develope into a whole spirit.

These supernatural beings are often sighted on the battlefield.

Some of the pictures given to me by various people have these orbs in them. Although Sack's Bridge is not on the battlefield, it is connected with the battle and the death of soldiers.

Ginny, who goes to the bridge with Tony, has had her hair pulled and her neck lightly touched. She has seen the orbs in the rafters of the bridge.

Many people claim to be touched by these earthly visitors.

Hildred, on one of her many visits to Gettysburg, has also seen a soldier standing on the bridge. The bridge seems to be a "hot spot" of activity for our ghostly visitors from the other side.

This is a perfect example of orbs. This was taken on a clear night inside of Sach's Bridge.

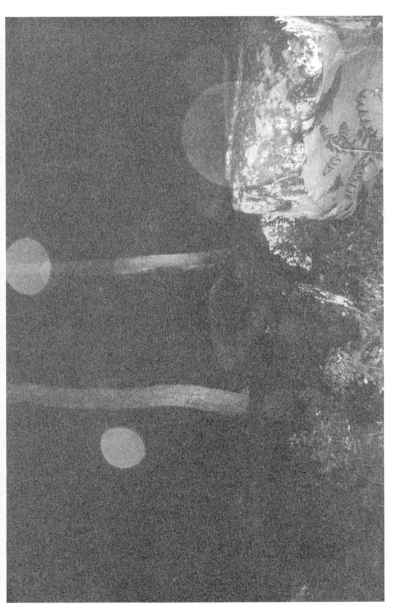

This picture was taken by Wendy Johnson. This is a field hospital on the loop.

GENERAL PICKETT

T O

GENERAL ROBERT E. LEE

(AFTER THE BATTLE OF PICKETT'S CHARGE ON JULY 3RD)

"WITH BITTERNESS GENERAL LEE, I HAVE NO DIVISION NOW."

ORBS OF MY OWN

After hearing of so many encounters with Rebel spirits, I finally decided to experiment with them. Asking my husband to wear his Union General uniform, we headed for the bridge. He really felt silly walking around the bridge in uniform at night and he was opposed to the idea but, he was shocked at the response he received.

We could hear men talking very plainly but, could not make out what they were saying.

I decided to get pictures and nothing was going to stop me. I will admit, I was greatly frightened.

We heard a few unexplainable noises, but we were not deterred.

As I snapped a few shots, I clearly heard someone walking on the bridge. Shining the flashlight about, I saw no one.

The feeling of not being alone hit us both at the same time.

We decided that the Rebs had had enough of this Union officer. We left before we got really scared.

I was very excited when I found an orb eyeball to eyeball with my husband.

My husband Ed at Sach's Bridge. He and the orb are eye to eye.

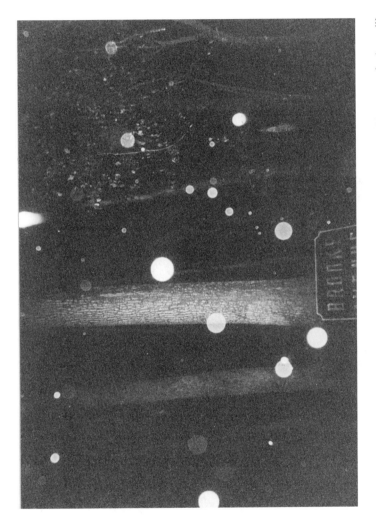

Suzanne Row of Three Mile. Pa. took this while walking along Brook Ave. Unaware of what will appear on her film, Suzanne has an uncanny talent for capturing the unseen on her camera.

EAST CAVALRY FIELD

COLONEL MCINTOSH-

SHOUTING AT THE MICHIGANDER,

"FOR GOD'S SAKE MEN, IF YOU ARE

EVER GOING TO STAND, STAND NOW.

FOR YOU ARE ON YOUR FREE SOIL!"

I was very excited to receive these next two pictures from Betty Estelow of Delanco, New Jersey.

Betty took these pictures last summer and just got them developed.

The first picture is my husband Ed Matusiak, who portrays General Winfield Scott Hancock, with an unknown re-enactor.

This picture was taken below the Chamberlain Monument. Notice the orb on Hancock's belt buckle.

Another unusual occurrence that seems to appear in a lot of pictures is a mysterious pink streak. This seems to happen quite often when there are re-enactors about as you can see on pages 138 & 139.

REYNOLD'S WOODS
JULY 1, 1863

A COLOR-BEARER OF THE 13TH NORTH CAROLINA, SUDDENLY HAD HIS RIGHT ARM TORN FROM THE SOCKET BY AN ARTILLERY SHELL. THE BLOODY YOUTH HARDLY PAUSED BUT, SHIFTED THE FLAG TO THE OTHER ARM AND BOUNDED FORWARD, SHOUTING, "FORWARD, FORWARD!"

My husband Ed and I were doing some research on the 24th Michigan. A hard fighting outfit of the Iron Brigade, serving under John Reynolds who was killed on the first day of the battle.

The pictures I took were of Reynolds Woods where the Iron Brigade lost more that half of their forces.

After snapping a few pictures of the woods, we left. Imagine the jolt it gave me when I started going threw the pictures and found the following one with not one, but two faces looking at me. There is also an orb on the tree.

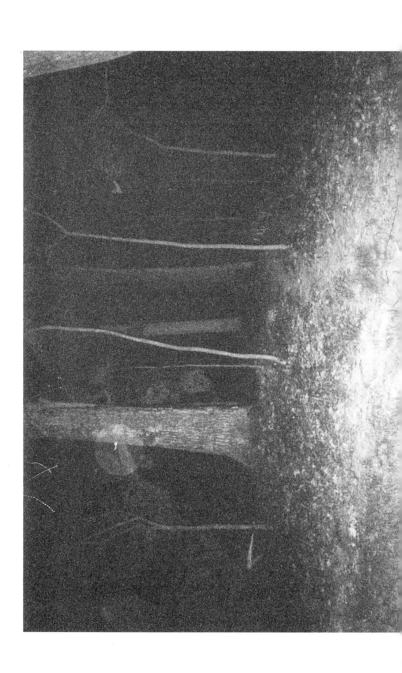

Reynold's Woods.

This monument sits in front of the field hospital. Below the Monument of the 5th Mich. sits a perfect round orb.

GETTYSBURG JULY 1, 1863

*A FEDERAL SHELL EXPLOED ON HERRS
RIDGE. A FRAGMENT SCRATCHED A
CAPTAIN'S HEAD PRODUCING BLOOD.
THE CAPTAIN RAN TO THE REAR
SHOUTING, "I'M DEAD, I'M DEAD. THE
COLONAL CALMY CALLED THE TWO
STRETCHER BEARERS. "GO TAKE THAT
DEAD MAN OFF-
IF YOU CAN CATCH HIM."*

I have had the honor of meeting a few psychics in my lifetime.

The one reading that I had with Karyol Kirkpatrick, was one of the most exciting and accurate readings that I have ever had.

Karyol told me that I would write and publish a book. Unknown to her, I had been working on this book!!

Although I cannot go into the whole reading, Karyol was not proven wrong on anything that she told me.

If anyone cares to contact Karyol, just call her for an appointment. She also does readings by phone. I feel you will not be disappointed.

Karyol probably knows more about the spirits that roam Gettysburg than anyone I have met so far.

Karyol Kirkpatrick
1-717-393-8827

Three Yankee re-enactors who posed at Sach's Bridge noticed the pink line running through their picture.

My husband, also at the bridge dressed as General Hancock.

1863

*GENERAL GEORGE MEAD, FROM
PHILADELPHIA, WAS PUT AT THE HEAD
OF THE ARMY OF THE POTOMAC BY
PRESIDENT ABRAHAM LINCOLN.*

*LINCOLN'S COMMENT: "LET HIM FIGHT
ON HIS OWN DUNG HILL!"*

The following picture is of Burnside Bridge at Antietam Battlefield. It appears that they have the same eerie orbs that are found in the pictures taken at Gettysburg. Sandy Olsen of Chambersburg, Pa. gave me this picture to show that they still roam on other battlefields as well. Look for more of Sandy's pictures in "The Battlefield Dead II".

Burnside Bridge

THROUGH A CHILD'S EYES

I started this book with one of my own experiences, and I will end it with one.

I was out taking pictures of the woods on the southern side of East Cavalry Field, where historians say there are still bodies buried. It was a beautiful sunny day in September. I had my daughter and my four year old grandson with me. I was back in the woods snapping pictures while Andrew and Wendy stood out on the road.

I was working my way back to the road when I stopped because I thought I heard someone walking with me.

As I stood there listening, my grandson called, "Gammom, come mer." Walking out to him, I asked what he wanted. "Gammom, there was a man standing by you and he had a wong gun."

It is said that children and animals may see and hear more because their minds are so clear and innocent.

Knowing Andrew as I do, I knew his innocent mind could not have made this up. I have a certain bond with this child, we are very close. I've taught him since he was old enough to talk, about God, lying and stealing. So when I asked him what the man looked like and what he was doing, I believe he told me exactly what he saw. This is his story:

He had a Civil War hat on and a wong gun, but he was fuzzy. I think he meant cloudy or see through. He said the soldier was not looking at me, but out at the field.

He was too young to know that General Custer fought on the other side of the field that he was pointing to.

I asked, "Where is the soldier now?", and he told me that he just "misappeared."

Walking back to the woods, I looked around but, saw nothing. I hit a cold spot (icy cold) and called to my daughter to come over to where I was. I backed away from the spot and instantly felt the warmth of the day return.

As Wendy walked through the cold spot, she rubbed her arms, saying "Wow, it's cold back here."

We stood there looking around the woods and Andrew said, "Gammom, that's where the man was," pointing at the cold spot we had just passed through.

This completely unnerved me. I took his little hand and we three headed back to town.